From University Graduate to

Master of the Universe

From University Graduate to

Master of the Universe

Strategies for Launching a Global Professional Career

By

Jasper S. Kim, Bliss Burdett Pak and Eugene Yun

Ewha Womans University Press

Master of the Universe
By Jasper S. Kim, Bliss Burdett Pak and Engene Yun

First published 15 December, 2006
Published by Ewha Womans University Press
11-1 Daehyun-dong, Seodaemun-gu, Seoul, Korea 120-750
Tel. (82-2)3277-3164, 362-6076
Fax. (82-2)312-4312
E-mail: press@ewha.ac.kr
Online Bookstore: http://www.ewhapress.com

price: 10,000won / U.S.$10.00

ISBN 89-7300-714-9 93320

Foreword

This volume is dedicated to Professor Jang Hee Yoo, in commemoration of his leadership and inspiration to the students of Ewha Womans University Division of International Studies and Graduate School of International Studies as Professor and founding Dean.

We owe many thanks to our students and colleagues from Ewha Womans University Division of International Studies and Graduate School of International Studies who participated in this project. Special thanks to Wonseok Woo, Ph.D., for his knowledgeable advice and to Brendan Howe, Ph.D., and Devin Joshi, A.B.D., for their valuable insights and recommendations. Special thanks also to Rebecca Kim, MeeYeong Kim and Yoon-Jeong Kim for their excellent transcriptions from our Q&A sessions. Thanks also to our alumni speakers at Ewha GSIS/DIS's Global Career Forum on May 16, 2006 who shared the "Things I Wish I Knew Before My First Job" for purposes of the Forum and this publication: Hannah Hee-kyung Jun, Jung Joo Seo, Soon Young Joo, Hee Kyoung Jeon and Bo Young Hwang. Last but not least, a heartfelt thanks and best wishes in their global careers to our students. We were particularly lucky to have participating students who were unafraid to offer their open, honest, entertaining and probing questions: Ellie Bae, Wendie Kim, EJ Shin, Eura Kim, Professor Jasper Kim's students in Autumn 2005 and Winter 2005, and Professor Bliss Burdett Pak's students in Autumn 2005.

Contents

Part I
Overview

Chapter 1 Introduction

This career guide is the product of Q&A sessions among the authors and groups of students participating in international studies programs at Ewha Womans University in Seoul, Korea. The content reflects the interests, concerns and challenges that every graduating senior faces in deciding what to do after graduation – and what greater career plan that first step implies. We invite you to relax and begin your life-long professional adventures with this Q&A conversation as an early step in the process. As you read the questions asked by university students in this project, you will likely see that there are many common concerns. As you read the answers and find that you need to know more – maybe a lot more – then we advise you turn to the "Resources" we provide at the end of each section of the book (many of which are also available for free on the Internet). Above all, it is best to keep your humor and good spirits as you set out on your post-university life's experience. Give yourself plenty of credit for having accomplished great things thus far in your life (you are about to graduate from a well-respected university, aren't you?) and pursue your greatest ambitions with all your heart. Expect success. You can achieve it by preparing yourself for the professional roles you wish to pursue. Consult the many resources around you, both those recommended in this book and those provided by your university, its faculty, career planning staff and alumni.

Lastly, be flexible and be ready to respond to change in our fast-moving, globally-integrated professional environments. Plan responsibly and take control of your own future. Be prepared to return to questions of planning and developing your career continuously over the two-to-four or possibly more decades that your professional career will span. It's your life, and you're just starting out on your post-graduate path. Which road will you take? We hope our guidance is helpful in navigating your early steps on whichever path you choose, and wish you a future full of personal and professional rewards.

Our Audience

The questions asked and answered here are taken from real, live conversations we had with our students. These students have a broad, international perspective for their careers. The authors are faculty members with backgrounds in business, economics, finance and law. The information provided here should be helpful to students at any major university who are planning a professional career with a global scope. The students asking the questions were international studies majors at Ewha Womans University in Seoul, Korea. Our goal is to be accessible to everyone, while on the other hand we do recognize our limitations. Therefore, many of our answers apply to the issues that are familiar to us, and reflect the problems we see as professors teaching here in Northeast Asia in the early twenty-first century. We believe the samples of questions apply broadly to anyone thinking about their careers immediately following university graduation – especially students with a global perspective.

The Q&A Format

We use the Q&A format to keep this reading light and to make it practical. We do not intend to be comprehensive. Much of our information is biased, based on our individual experiences as lawyers, investment bankers, M.B.A. graduates, Ph.D.'s, etc. For example, one of us said, "I don't really see any need for anyone to go to law school" while the other two of us who did go to law school have a quite different perspective about that! Readers should recognize that this is not the final say on the subjects covered here, but it may be a great place to start sorting out the issues and options available to graduating students. It should be one of the first things that they read in the grand project of finding their way out into the professional world beyond university. So the questions range from very easy, very basic, and very general, to sometimes quite specific and quite difficult. Some questions may not have clear or easy answers, but we present an approach for thinking them through. Here you have it: all you ever wanted to know about career management but were afraid to ask··· until today!

Chapter 2 What Are My Options After Graduation?

"'Would you tell me please which way I have to go from here?' 'That depends a good deal on where you want to get to,' said the cat."

– Lewis Carroll, *Alice's Adventures in Wonderland*

Q1: What are my options? After I graduate from college, what are my choices?

A1: Your choices are many and wide-ranging. They fall into three general categories: (i) going to work, (ii) continuing your formal education at the graduate level, or (iii) other, which may include volunteer roles, international travel, pursuing self-study for professional credentials (such as the Certified Public Accountant or Foreign Service exam or national equivalent) or technical skills, or various entrepreneurial endeavors.

Q2: If I study subject A, how does that affect my ability to get a job in field B (a different subject, maybe even unrelated to subject A)?

A2: Depending on the country of the undergraduate degree, your exact concentration may or may not be important. For example, for many of the U.S. schools and jobs, the major itself is not the primary concern. Therefore, you could do an undergraduate degree in philosophy and become a fund manager; or you could be a major in industrial design and end up going to theological school. I think the situation is a little more rigid in Asian markets. In Korea, for some reason employers care more about which major you have chosen for yourself as an undergraduate. Your next step out of university may be influenced by the undergraduate degree that you have completed if the position requires a background in the field. If you do not want to pursue the field in which you majored in university, look for a position that accepts applicants with a variety of educational backgrounds, such as banking, consulting and management trainee programs.

Q3: If I study subject A, how does that affect my ability to go to graduate school in field B (a different subject, maybe even unrelated to subject A)?

A3: Unlike the job-search requirements, there is very little linkage between the undergraduate degree and graduate degree when it comes to attending graduate school in the social sciences and humanities. However, for hard sciences or technical fields, there are specific undergraduate requirements or recommendations – e.g., math, chemistry, economics (math requirements), etc. At the undergraduate level, my view is that broader is better than narrower, simply because a broad education gives you more options.

Starting from your undergraduate education, you can think of your career as a pyramid. A pyramid is broad at the base and narrows incrementally toward the top. The first layer of that pyramid is your foundation: it is critically important, and it should give you a broad foundation. That is why a liberal arts curriculum, social sciences (such as history, politics or economics) or a multi-disciplinary international studies undergraduate education are examples of a good start. These types of broad education expose you to many different subjects. Among those subjects, you may choose to focus on one in graduate school or in your early professional life. If the first graduate field or job you choose is not a good fit for your longer-term career for some reason, then you have a broad educational base that prepares you for other fields as well. You can recalibrate your career later if your foundation is solid.

Q4: If I am graduating from college with a good general education but not specific marketable skills, how do I decide which field I should go into now?

A4: If they can afford it, many students who have a broad liberal arts or social sciences background find it beneficial to go to graduate school and study for a Master's degree in order to help them do some filtering, and to deepen their knowledge in a particular direction. For example, an "international studies" background is both a blessing and a curse because it forms a quality base for your pyramid; read on to examine your options for the next level.

Q5: My university degree is in political science and diplomacy. For what types of graduate school programs in the United States would I be qualified to attend? Which would benefit me over the course of my professional career?

A5: There are several options available to you. First of all, there are Master's degree programs in international relations. Law school and public policy programs would also be interested in someone with your background. An M.B.A. is also possible if you are willing to work for several years before you go to graduate school. Another option is of course to study for a Ph.D. in political science or a related field such as history.

Q6: What kinds of skills do I have as a freshly-minted college graduate? Do I need to develop specific skills to offer an employer?

A6: When a company hires a fresh graduate – or when they hire anyone without job experience – they don't expect a particular set of technical skills to come with that person in most cases. You should not worry that you do not know enough accounting or economic theory. Companies are looking for common sense. They are looking for good communication skills, your ability to be a team player, attitude and enthusiasm. These are general things that we can expect out of anyone. In selecting the new hires, the interviewers are asking, "Does this person have a greater degree of interest than the next candidate?" "Does this person seem to be better-informed?" "Has she researched our company well?" "Does he have a more realistic idea of what's important to our company than the next person?" Being able to solve one more technical question is not what most employers are looking for. You and every other new graduate will be similarly situated in terms of lacking technical skills relevant to the day-to-day work at the company. The company plans to teach you how to do things their way, so specific skills should not be your major concern. Everyone is in the same shoes in terms of inexperience due to your age and stage of life.

Q7: How do companies distinguish among all these inexperienced candidates who are all going after the same jobs?

A7: They are looking for the potential to add value. Their choice is ultimately a function of your attitude as much as other traits. You need to have the willingness to be proactive, to learn and to contribute. Wherever you work, you will be in a new environment. You have to learn the ropes, work hard and be happy doing it (not grumbling about long hours or hating the environment). Your approach should be, "here is a problem and I am here to provide solutions; I can do it and I am happy to do it – that's why I am here." It's this problem-solving ability and the willingness to work through new problems, new facts and new situations that companies seek.

Q8: When should I start thinking about my next move after my undergraduate degree – in my junior year or senior year? When is a good time to start?

A8: Students these days start quite early. Some of them start when they are freshmen, trying to manage their education towards a career. They choose educational experiences that will look good on their resumes. However, concerns for post-graduate life should not overshadow the learning and opportunities in terms of life experience that are unique to the undergraduate years. As you make decisions about what to major in and how to spend your summers, it is smart to consider the quality of the experience you are getting for the time spent, and how it will influence your future options.

Part II
The First Professional Job

Chapter 3 Professional Options

Congratulations!
Today is your day.
You're off to Great Places!
You're off and away!

– Dr. Seuss, *Oh, the Places You'll Go!*

Q1: Which entry-level positions offer the best opportunities for learning and professional development? I'm so afraid of taking a dead-end job that will be all grunt work and no personal development!

A1: Every professional environment will provide an opportunity to develop new skills. Any first job forms a platform for you to build a network of personal and professional contacts, and offers insights into the workplace and the industry. Your personal development is unlikely to be stunted in the first job. It is more likely that you will be challenged simply because it is your first time in a full-time professional position. The returns from your first year or two in terms of experience will be relatively high. After this initial period of getting your feet wet, there is the possibility that you will begin to experience decreasing marginal returns. For example, if you are not moving up the chain of command in the company or somehow taking on additional responsibility, you may see that the position's potential to take you to the next level is limited. At this point, you should look within the company for promotion opportunities and discuss the "decreasing returns" situation with your manager. Also, look outside your company for possible lateral moves to a job at a different organization. Finally, consider graduate school for a jump-start to your progression.

Q2: What are the signals of a good first job and a bad first job? What kinds of questions should I ask in the interview to try to assess the quality of the work involved with the position?

A2: As long as the position is a professional one with a promotion track, you should not be too picky about the work you are asked to do. Your first job is all about getting some experience in a high-quality workplace. The better the employer's reputation, the more complex and sophisticated the work that is produced there, and thus the more likely your entry-level job is going to involve a good deal of "grunt work."

What is grunt work? It is work you are capable of doing, and need to learn to do well and efficiently, while you are absorbing the priorities and subtleties of your new employer's business. It is document production, summarizing, reviewing, editing, number-crunching, researching, brainstorming, staying up late to make sure a project makes a deadline, and the like. It is the difficult and less-than-glamorous part of work. If you do it well and with a good attitude, you can learn a lot. Better yet, you can gain the trust of your seniors and next year when the new class arrives in your department, you may be supervising them as they help out with the grunt work and you move to a higher level. With any luck, you will have mastered the art of executing projects and be competent and trustworthy in your next higher spot on the "food chain." Do not worry – grunt work is not an insult; it is a relatively low-risk way for you to learn the business. We all are lucky if we start out like the

Karate Kid: "wax on, wax off" (i.e., build your basic strength first; hone the fighting skills later).

Q3: What kind of job can I get in a big firm? I have a social science major, so I know a lot about history and politics, and I took some economics courses and one finance course. What kind of job am I eligible for?

A3: Many companies have training programs and are not looking for a particular skill set like engineering. They're looking for a smart person. Some examples of these kinds of firms are accounting firms (though they will want some business background); consulting firms (which hire people from a variety of undergraduate majors); investment banks; companies' management track positions; and research positions at think tanks or political organizations. These employers are looking for problem-solving ability and your ability to think on your feet. These firms use proxy information to assess your abilities: grades, awards and other achievements including extra-curricular activities like debate or publications – anything that provides evidence of a sharp mind and the will to succeed.

Q4: I'm not sure I'm interested in working just to make money. I was active in social and environmental action groups during college, and I would like to pursue related fields in my professional life. What are my options?

A4: High quality work is available in your areas of interest at non-profit organizations and various types of research institutions (ranging from public and private universities, specialized institutes with public or private funding, think tanks, and various kinds of advocacy groups). You also will find significant amounts of charitable work, community-oriented projects and environmental management efforts being carried on inside the better companies around the world. To identify these companies, look for things like a Corporate Citizenship or Corporate Social Responsibility or Sustainability report on the company's website. Over 800 companies now produce Sustainability Reports under the Global Reporting Initiative (www.globalreporting.org) and generally allocate resources to these efforts within the company or through their related foundations.

As with any potential employer, you must research both the funding and political nature of the institution to make sure its purposes fit with yours. Both public and private grant money is available in some fields to organizations that are not profit-oriented. Just because the organization is not run for shareholders' profit does not mean it is unable to pay reasonably well for high quality professionals; it depends entirely on the nature of the organization, the nature of the work, the funding sources, etc. Be aware that an organization that does not fund its own operations by turning a profit is dependent on its funding sources for its continued existence. In the twenty-first century, vast amounts of wealth have been donated to charitable foundations around the world to fund research and other work that does not get done (or done well or delivered adequately) by the for-profit sector. See the Resources at the end of this section for International Organizations, Global Social Work and NGO resources to begin your search.

Q5: I have a question about the departments I might work in. I've heard that I should apply directly to the department where I am seeking the position. How much does the department where I work affect my general career path?

A5: Your choice of first job and initial department assignment may have a significant impact. They certainly point you in a certain direction on your career path. It is quite normal for companies to have several career paths, and your trajectory depends on where you have come into the organization. To get into sales, you may need technical experience first. To move into a management role, you may need to begin in a management trainee program. It may be impossible or highly unusual for an administrative staff position to lead you into a management or sales position (or anything other than the support staff role). Look for departments that are the cash-cow for the company: where are their profit centers? Are you in an essential function at the company? If you can be replaced by a machine or anyone who is awake during your shift, you are not in a good position to grow.

Q6: Is my first job my job for life? Can I relax when I finally get the first job offer?

A6: Usually not. Normally, you would not expect to stay at one company from the beginning to your retirement in the modern world. With a government career track, you may be able to advance through the ranks of the agency throughout a career – governments tend not to go out of business or merge as frequently as private companies. Life-long employment with the same firm is less common in this day and age. As you enter the labor force, you should be figuring on working for several companies throughout your career, and taking on many different tasks. Change is the norm now, and no organization can guarantee you that it will be around for your entire career – at least not in its current form – much less offer you a job for life. If they do, run away; that company's managers are not being honest with you or themselves.

Q7: What are the consequences of switching departments within a company or firm?

A7: If you are a poor worker, then whichever department you go to, they will try to get rid of you as quickly as possible. In that case, you will find yourself switching departments quite regularly! If you are a very good worker, then other departments will want you. In that case, you will also find yourself switching positions quite regularly as well. The key is to switch into a better (higher-ranking, better-paid) position, leveraging your experience to date. It is a fact of professional life that there is frequent change in staffing, and we know that in some companies they like to rotate their employees around various departments to give them wider exposure. Take advantage of the additional learning this provides.

Q8: If I go into the sales department and then, after several years, I realize I have more interest in a different department, is it difficult to move to a different department within this company or should I look outside this company?

A8: If you are making any move, you should evaluate your options both inside and outside the company. You may get more credit for your experience inside the company where you already are known and the new department values your firm-specific knowledge. You may be able to get the best promotion by making the in-company move. But it may go the other way: you may want to make an outside move to get to a different industry with better prospects, or into a different working atmosphere. A decision to move should be checked against the opportunity cost of the other options available to you at the decision time. There's no excuse for being lazy and sticking your head in the sand.

Q9: Is it disloyal to research salaries and job opportunities in my field, even after I have started working for a particular firm or company?

A9: No, it is your duty as a self-respecting, intelligent human being. Every year you stay with a certain organization in a certain role, there is the opportunity cost of the other things you could be doing over that period. A decision not to regularly evaluate the market and your other job options is not loyalty, it is deliberate ignorance. If your employer wants to keep you, they also will stay current on employment terms and conditions in the market and compete with other potential employers to keep you happy. They may not tell you this is what they are doing, but there is plenty of evidence that employers step up to meet labor market terms if they want to attract the best candidates and compete with other firms for talent.

Your employer will not inform you of what your alternatives are, but you should talk to other people working in your field and in similar positions. Websites are chock full of shared information among employees (see Resources at the end of this section). Your decision to stay in a job or to change your job should be an informed decision. As the saying goes, even if you choose not to decide you still have made a choice. So you should always make well-informed choices. Just make sure to do the research on your own time at home, not on the company's computer.

Q10: Is it a good idea to change jobs regularly?

A10: Do not change jobs just for a change of scenery. Do not change jobs too often or you start to appear as a job-hopper and unreliable in the eyes of the next potential employer. Think in terms of three to five years as a normal range for spending in one position, with one company. Plan to leverage your experience to move up the employee food chain when you do make a change.

Q11: What if I want to work for a big multinational corporation? How do I navigate all their departments – marketing, finance, sales, human resources, etc.? How do I know which positions are on a track for advancement within the company and the industry?

A11: Whenever you think about finding work at a company or any organization, you must start with researching your target employer and finding out all you can about how the place works. Who are the decision-makers? What direction is the company moving? Where are its high-growth and profitable areas?

If you like competition, go into the most highly sought-after departments. Those are usually the departments where the most action is, and they are the most highly-regarded within that company. If you do well there, then you rise to stardom (or at least your promotions are much better). For example, in a fund management company, it's a good idea to be a fund manager. In a marketing company, it's good to be in the marketing front line and not in the accounting department (unless you are looking to remain an accountant). Identify where the action should be, given the company's business.

Q12: I hear these strange things about working in a "cubicle." Isn't office life unbearable if you have to work in such a boring space?

A12: It's not the cubicle that's the problem. If someone is unhappy at work, it's probably something else, and the "cubicle" environment is a kind of proxy to blame. Maybe they're getting paid too little; maybe they're not getting recognition. People say, "I don't want to get stuck in a cubicle," but I think that it's not the physical environment they are really complaining about. Don't shun away from jobs that put you in a cubicle but identify what is it that an unhappy employee really doesn't like: Is it the close space? Is it the lack of money? Is it the fact that no one comes to say hello to me – that I have no friends or I think I have no life? Once you've analyzed the real factors and fixed the real problem, you may decide that this cubicle is great! It lets me see all these movies on the Internet and I can chat with my friends; I can eat whatever food I want to; I can take my shoes off and no one complains – there are a lot of things to consider about a cubicle!

Q13: What if I dislike fierce competition and seek something more stable and comfortable in my professional life?

A13: You may opt to go to departments where there is less competition. I strongly believe that there is a great deal of happiness to be found where there is not too much competition. Look for departments that rely on a special skill set. After you have developed that skill set, it will be hard for them to replace you. Look for departments where turnover is low and people do not seem to be burning out at a young age. Look for areas of the company that have long-term relevance and are a necessary function of the company. If pressure bothers you, find a place where there is a steady work flow instead of project-based work that can run up against stiff deadlines. Where there is less client exposure, generally there is less direct pressure. However, you should be aware that less pressure usually indicates less upward mobility and probably lower pay, and less decision-making power at the company over the longer term.

Q14: Is it better to go to a small company in a professional position, or is it more important to get a big firm name on my resume, even if the only job available to me is described as support staff or secretarial?

A14: Generally speaking, starting your career at a prestigious firm is relevant only if you are working as a professional there. You would not apply for a good M.B.A. program on the basis of work experience as a secretary or copy center employee. You are far better off in a professional position at a smaller or less-known firm than taking a support staff position at a big name company. But big name companies should not be interviewing university graduates for jobs that require only a high school diploma, and you should not apply for such a job. Look far and wide for the best job for which you are qualified.

Q15: What's the difference between "professional" and "support staff"?

A15: "Professional" positions imply that a certain level of education is a prerequisite (which you now have, with your university Bachelor's degree), and a certain amount of responsibility comes with the position. In exchange for a responsible position in the company, you are more highly compensated and given more challenging work. Your professional job is more likely to involve exercising judgment, taking responsibility for profit/loss or performance of your unit or team, engaging in creative or problem-solving work rather than merely following instructions.

Non-professionals may be defined as the group of people providing support in various office functions, such as word processing, order processing, answering phones or mail, and myriad other functions which mostly require doing a specific function in response to clear instructions from the management-level folks. The nature of both professional and support or clerical work at any company will differ, based on the business. For example, at a manufacturing plant, there are different roles played by the employees on the factory floor who are skilled in operating machinery, the administrative office staff and management people who decide on strategy, pricing, expansion, finance and managing client relationships.

Q16: I think I'm interested in business or banking. How should I prepare to interview with these kinds of firms?

A16: Take some accounting, basic economics and finance courses if you have time for them. No matter where you go initially (even if you don't think you'll be in business), you should take accounting and economics courses as a matter of general literacy in the workplace. These are high value-added subjects. Internships during university are helpful, too. A rough guess is that maybe 20% of the actual work you do in a business job involves things you learned at school. The rest of your role is based on basic human skills such as communication and time management. Even if you do not get a good grade in your accounting or finance class, you should not worry too much, because these things happen. Chances are you will do fine, the math will not hurt too much and you will see great rewards for the time you invested in these basic "how the world works" kind of courses.

Q17: What is banking all about? Is it just about money? Do bankers have a reputation for being money hungry?

Q17: Well, sure, profits are the point of the business. The interesting part is how to earn them. It is about working with clients and being of service, bringing value to the clients.

Q18: Investment banking sounds exciting. What area of banking firms is the best place to look for a first job? Are there many women in banking these days?

A18: It is important to understand what part of an investment bank you would like to work in. Actually, banks remain somewhat male-dominated in the investment banking division where they advise on mergers, acquisitions and finance deals (though recent lawsuits and large damages awards in the U.S. for discrimination in promotions and hostile workplace suits have created some sensitivity to the issues at global institutions). You can, of course, turn the majority-male situation to your advantage if you are female: you'll naturally stand out from the crowd. This helps get you noticed at client meetings. Of course, you must be prepared for the issues such a situation raises as well (entertainment culture, golf course deal-making, etc.). Like anywhere else, you must choose your personal style. In banking or other business settings, it never hurts to be a decent golfer.

Equity research requires you to become an industry specialist and research companies – there you can carve out a niche for yourself. Sales and trading is an entirely different field that is fast-paced and rewards calculated risk-taking (a successful year can be very well rewarded indeed). Check out the firms' websites (see the list of Resources at end of this section) and see how diversified they are. Many banks operate as full-service financial institutions, owning many businesses and situated in a global network of locations.

Q19: What's the difference between the "front office" and "back office" at an investment bank? Which is a better place to work?

A19: Most investment banks are different from commercial banks: they take different views of the market and can either make a lot of money or lose a lot of money. As a result of that type of approach, it has a very competitive, relatively stressful working environment but with the highest potential pay for success. Within investment banks, there is a basic division between the front office and the back office. The front office is usually comprised of trading (with various specialties such as bond trading, equity traders, commodities traders, etc.); a sales force (who act as a bridge between the outside investors and the internal traders); research analysts (also a profit center); and specialized investment bankers (handling mergers and acquisitions, underwriting securities). The back office is mostly administrative people who support the money-makers' operations: treasury, finance, lawyers, internal auditors and others. The front office people are at the top of the food-chain because firm profits are created by what they do. If the front office says "jump," then the back office will jump. If they say jump higher, the back office will jump higher because the business is driven by the front office and their clients.

Q20: What's a good job?

A20: Do you really expect us to say something like investment banking or management consulting, or joining an NGO to change the world? We won't (not here, anyway). You've asked a really tough question. Here's one answer: the best job is a job that you really like. It's not a job at a particular company; it's not defined by where you are or who you belong to. These superficial descriptions do not tell you what makes a good job. Jobs at the world's best-known, most prestigious organizations can be a horrible fit and a terrible job for a particular individual, but great for another person. The answer is inside of you. Don't take a job that your parents want you to have, or that your friends would like to do. Your talent is much too valuable for that. Do something that you like. I wish I had known that when I was graduating.

Chapter 4 Global Mobility

Q1: Many students consider trying to get a job overseas. What are the advantages or disadvantages for students who were educated in Asia, in trying to get a job outside their home country? If I do get the job, what are the advantages and disadvantages that I can expect in working in the overseas work force?

A1: There are benefits to overseas jobs. The first is that the foreign job may pay a higher salary than in your home country. The second is that for women, there may be less of a glass ceiling. The third may be mobility in terms of moving across the divisions of a company, meaning that being promoted may be based on your merits rather than your personal connections. The downside is that you need certain special attributes, such as language skills. English is the first among them. In an increasingly global environment, I think English and at least one or two other languages are recommended. For example, students in Korea should speak and write well in English and Korean, and also Japanese or Mandarin Chinese.

Q2: If I want to work in a foreign country, should I look for a place where there are many expatriates from my home country? Is this the way to get connected there?

A2: Fellow countrymen can be a great connection in a foreign market. Do not limit yourself to following the herd, however. Look for your own competitive angle: what do you have that uniquely qualifies you for a certain job in a certain place? You may want to distinguish yourself from the crowd of your compatriots.

For example, in terms of languages, a company will look for language ability that is needed in markets to which it plans to expand. Companies are likely to hire candidates with language abilities that are different from what they've already got in the firm. So an American firm with many Korean-speaking employees is not particularly drawn to hiring a Korean-American who speaks English and Korean to work at their office in the U.S. However, they may be very interested to hire the same person if she speaks Mandarin and is willing to work in China. Likewise, a Korean and English speaker may have more of a competitive advantage working elsewhere in Asia, not in Seoul or the U.S., based on their English and Korean language and cultural familiarity.

Q3: Which places are considered the "global marketplace?" Are there two or three top cities?

A3: The global marketplace is now any major financial center. There are a growing number of these. A basic definition would include a large amount of business flowing through the city, and productive financial activity taking place there. Given the global mobility of capital and people, the best cities to live and work in have increasingly less dependence on a large local consumer population, natural resources and native son favoritism (though you can't rule this out entirely, of course). The most successful financial centers are based on quality of life for the people who choose to live there, quality of law and quality of professional services available there. Examples include Singapore, Hong Kong, Beijing, Shanghai, Tokyo, New York, London, Paris, other European capitals, Dubai, Mumbai and New Delhi. You should consider the many places where employers seek young talent and pay well for it.

Q4: Is hiring and promotion usually based on personal connections, such as my family's reputation? Won't I lose this type of advantage if I work outside my hometown?

A4: In globally competitive companies overseas, the work environment is much more transparent than may be the norm in your home country or hometown. Your family name, the prestige of your early education, and the socio-economic status of your neighborhood are likely to be unknown or less relevant in a foreign city. Whether this is a plus or a minus for you, you may find that you benefit personally simply from the overseas living experience. You may gain a great deal of confidence, among other personal rewards, from learning on the job and being rewarded based on performance rather than personal favors or tenure.

If your home market hires and promotes based on identity and age, you will likely see a major difference in a major financial center, where companies live and die based on their profitability. Profitability is greatly driven by the productivity of the work force, especially in professional firms. Therefore, company management measures productivity and builds incentive structures to reward the best employees. This means that as a young professional, you will primarily be reviewed according to objective factors on a regular basis (usually once or twice a year). You will receive feedback or constructive criticism at regular performance reviews and on an ad hoc (occasional) basis when needed. The system will resemble a meritocracy as closely as management can construct it.

Some people thrive in this environment and find the rewards to be fair and far-reaching, both in terms of professional advancement and financial advancement, while the work opportunity allows them (and their families) to live in a world-class city. Others find the meritocracy stressful and too uncertain in comparison with a more predictable work environment they can expect in companies in their home country.

Q5: Is it the norm for employees to be promoted based on seniority at large multinational firms?

A5: A professional position will start you on a career track. Seniority plays a very important role in the early stages until you have a track record for success or, a-hem, something less. At some companies (in Asian countries especially), seniority may continue to determine your role at the company over your entire career. In Western-style companies, merit is often measured by objective criteria, and promotions are made on an individual basis rather than a seniority basis. In these firms, you need to have a clear idea of the criteria on which you will be judged. Most likely this list of merit factors will be provided to you, along with constructive criticism and an assessment of how you are doing on a regular basis (often around the end of the year or bonus time).

Q6: What advantages do I have based on my native ethnicity and culture? How can I leverage this advantage internationally in looking for a job?

A6: Let's use the example of a Korean graduating senior conducting a job search at major cities in Asia. There are clear advantages to being Korean: first of all, you bring to your employer your expertise from Korea – this may be a much deeper knowledge of Korea than other candidates, and may be knowledge that is generally applicable to the Asian region. The current century has been called the age of the Pacific Rim. I believe that your knowledge of this region, and Korea, will be quite important to employers looking for this kind of background. On whole, Koreans have a good reputation for working extremely hard and for being smart. These are the things that you want to utilize. If a good reputation is already established, why not use it to your advantage?

Q7: What are the downsides to promoting my credentials as a person of a certain ethnicity? Can this be counter-productive, or come at a certain cost, if I play the ethnicity/nationality card?

A7: Continuing with the Korean example: if you are viewed as Korean or "from Asia" you may be labeled as an expert in this area right from the beginning. This may mean you do not get as wide a choice as you would like in terms of your specialty field in the early days. However, you are just starting out and you are looking to just get going in a certain field. Once you establish yourself on the team and prove yourself capable of handling a variety of issues, questions and problems, your talents will be recognized and you can widen your field over time.

An investment banking example of a sales and trading new hire: you may start out at the Korea desk, then move to the Saudi Arabia desk or Europe desk, and that may be a relatively natural and easy progression once you are an insider in the organization because you are known and trusted, and you will see the opportunities arising within the firm. What may at first seem somewhat limiting may work out over time, and you may need to use your special background to gain access to the general profession you wish to enter.

Q8: How do I get an overseas or far-away employer to believe that I really want to move to their city and build a career with their firm? Doesn't it just look like I want to visit as a tourist?

A8: It's not so far-fetched that you would be a valuable asset – you and the other few million global professionals who personally value their international living experience, and whose employers greatly benefit from having professional staff they can deploy to various regions of the world to take advantage of business opportunities there. Not all business can be home-grown, and companies are looking to hire globally mobile staff, so there is demand for your global services. In 2006, there was a significant shortage of finance professionals and high demand in Hong Kong, for example.

How do you prove you are globally mobile? You need to be able to explain in rational terms why you want to relocate. Your story needs to make personal and professional sense, both for your employer's and your own peace of mind. Why do you want to work there? Start with something other than "salaries are higher." Tie the place to the professional opportunity. Quality markets, training opportunities, great companies and other professionally-connected factors are a good start. Do some research and be ready to demonstrate your connection to the place. Spending time in that place as a student is an excellent way to start.

Q9: How long must I commit to working in an overseas position? Is there a contract I must sign?

A9: Employers of new graduates are planning to invest significant time and resources training their new hires. They expect to amortize that investment over some reasonable period of time, probably two or three years at a minimum. It is also in your best interest to keep your first job for at least a couple of years to establish a good track record as a reliable employee. There are of course exceptions to these general rules, but in general the best thing that a fresh graduate can demonstrate is dedication and success with their first job. With the two-three year time horizon in mind, both overseas companies and potential employees are looking at whether this makes any sense for them to agree on job terms. Contracts for overseas work are common, especially if the employer is paying any moving expenses (though expense reimbursements are less common for junior positions; moves are generally fully-paid for more senior employees and their families). Practically speaking, an employer cannot force you to stay in a work contract – that would be slavery, which is very unpopular nowadays. However, employers could possibly withhold pay or bill you for expenses they covered if you leave before your contract term.

Q10: Does it matter if I have never been to the place I want to work?

A10: Geography matters. If you as a student can establish some connection to the place where you would like to be, whether it's Paris or Singapore, you have much better chances of convincing an employer you are a rational risk. Spend a summer doing an internship there, or study abroad there for a semester or a year. Certainly, travel there as much as possible.

Contact industry groups or alumni who are there. Personal contacts are best; professional contacts of any nature are helpful. Your goal is to show that you have been there and you have a professional reason to be working there. Getting the geography story established is an absolute prerequisite to making a geographical move. Alumni from your university are a natural starting point for finding those contacts.

Q11: How do I handle the issue of getting a work visa? Will employers not consider me if I don't already have a visa?

A11: Working outside your home country always requires you to have a special permission from the host country – a work visa (which is different than a tourist visa or the right to travel there using just your passport). There are strict requirements you and your employer must meet to get a visa, so you need to find out what the rules are for the destination where you want to work. However, this is not your problem to handle entirely on your own: any well-established employer will walk you through the process and help you get the appropriate visa after they have decided to hire you. You have guessed correctly that some employers will not consider employees for whom they would have to get a visa, so mark them off your list of possible employers and move on. Most large companies, banks or intergovernmental organizations are accustomed to handling visa issues and they can sponsor the visa through their legal department or immigration person in-house. If they are set up to hire foreigners, they are set up to process your visa. If they seem unhelpful or uncertain as to how they will handle this basic legal requirement, this is a signal that they are not serious or well-equipped to hire foreigners; you should look carefully before signing on.

Chapter 5 Job Search Process

Q1: If I am about to go into the job market, when should I start contacting companies?

A1: Research your potential employer before you start contacting them. The earlier you start researching, the better. However, actually applying too early may not be beneficial. Your files may gather dust in some recruiting office if you do not wait until recruiting season to put your name in the hat. There are probably no advantages to applying too early – like six months earlier than the employer's recruiting schedule. It is important to find out what schedule the company is working with. In the case of foreign countries, the academic and company recruitment calendars may be altogether different than in your home country, so you must look into the seasonal set-up as well as the specific company's recruiting calendar. Then you can contact the recruiting department of the firm you're interested in, or an industry search firm.

Q2: How can I manage the supply and demand – the competitive environment – for the best jobs?

A2: In competing for jobs, there is supply and demand pressure on the decision. You can influence the demand for you in a positive way: choose to interview with several different companies within the same industry. Your interviewer will probably give you some opportunity to discuss what you are looking for in your career, and you can mention that you are focused on this industry and that you are in fact talking with companies w, x, y, and z – who happen to be the major competitors of this employer, both for clients and for recruits! This will serve two purposes. First, it demonstrates your sincere interest in the industry, and in the job for which you have applied with the firm. Second, going through the interview process with several leading companies in the field will educate you, so that you will be well-informed and have more success in your interviews on the whole.

If you want to be in consulting or telecommunications, go through several interviews with the top five consulting firms or the top tier of telecommunication companies in the city where you want to live. This also helps with the geography story (proving you really do want to live and work in this town, if it's not your hometown where you have family and other natural connections). You need not feel any loyalty to any one company until you have accepted an offer and gone to work for them. You may be sure they feel none to you until you are firmly on board with them.

Q3: I want to work for a large, multinational firm; however, most job listings at these firms require the candidates to have an M.B.A. or a J.D., or to have graduated from a top-tier school. It seems unfair that I don't seem to have much chance of getting the management track job I would like at one of these companies. What can I do?

A3: Every job has certain requirements as far as education level, experience and professional qualifications. If the job requires an

M.B.A. or a J.D. and you don't have one, do not waste your time applying for the job – you do not qualify. If you want to qualify, go out and get the credentials. You are likely to live and work for many decades. It takes relatively little time to obtain the graduate degrees and work experience to qualify you to move up into the role you would like for yourself.

Q4: Who is the decision maker at most companies or firms for candidate credentials and hiring decisions?

A4: Companies have profiles of the schools, grades and other credentials for the employee candidates they seek to hire. Senior managers develop the requirements for candidates and provide guidelines to their recruiters. The profile will limit the recruiters to certain educational pre-requisites or previous work experience pre-requisites, and sometimes to certain universities or licenses required in a field. The human resources or recruiting staff sift through resumes and sometimes post a listing to solicit candidates.

Many times, the solicitation begins inside the firm: the human resources office or hiring manager advertises to the department and other company employees that there is an opening for x position, asking them to forward candidates if they know anyone who would be interested and would fit well within the organization. Many positions are filled this way – based on direct recruitment by organization insiders rather than a public notice or formal search process. This is why it can be very helpful for you to build connections to people within the industry, profession and market in which you want to work, through personal connections, professional associations, alumni groups, industry groups – any activity through which you meet people in a position to think of you when there is demand for the type of position you seek.

Q5: I am a senior, and I have received an offer of full-time employment with a company – success! However, this company has asked me to leave school and start work there next week! What should I do?

A5: This is a very difficult position for you, but you must analyze it in terms of the long-term consequences for you. First, discuss this with your university career counselor. The university needs to be aware of this dilemma for your case and for others. If it is a good job and you don't want to lose it, you should make special arrangements with the university to complete your degree over an extended period of time or on an untraditional class schedule. This will of course require that you talk to all the professors and get their understanding. In Korea, our experience has been that the universities are supportive of students who land good jobs; they may be able to adjust coursework and schedules (such as setting exams for you), so that you can do it all. You will still have to earn your grades and your graduation.

The best option is for you to ask your company to hold that job until you complete your education. Chances are they will wait. Talk to them directly and realistically about your enthusiasm for the position. Offer to work part-time during the semester or for short-terms at summer and winter break until graduation day. Working and studying requires a great deal of coordination, but it's possible and it has been done to the student's benefit where the job offer is worth the effort. One way to cope with that situation is that these days there are many cyber courses. If you are only left with six or nine credits, you may be able to take two or three classes through the Internet. Do not simply stop attending class and expect mercy at exam time due to a job when you are still a student – work out a realistic plan with everyone concerned.

Q6: I just saw an advertisement for a job opening at ABC Company, and I would like to find out more about the company. What should I do?

A6: You pursue a two-track approach to assembling the relevant information. Track one: "outsider" information. Track two: "insider" information.

Track one is your basic research: start with the company's own web site, where you can see how they project their image. Large companies, especially publicly-traded ones and consumer-oriented ones, have large stores of information publicly available, including management names, values, major shareholders' identities, usually a message from the CEO, a statement about the values the company holds dear, suppliers, and investors. You may be able to get very detailed information like financial statements and strategies. Look especially for power point presentations by analysts posted on their websites under "investor relations:" these are presentations to the investment community which highlight growth areas and give you an overview of the whole company. You may be surprised to learn that what you thought was an oil company is actually a conglomerate in a dozen different industries, some of which are more profitable than others. If the company is publicly traded, you can go to the stock exchange web site and get their disclosure statements. Hoovers.com and the business press are good sources, too: search on the websites of *The International Herald Tribune, Business Week, Forbes, The Wall Street Journal* and *The Financial Times*. But do not stop there: get the insider view.

Once you have done your basic homework, talk to folks who know the company first-hand. Talk to people who are actually working at that company now, or were recently. A five minute conversation with someone who works in the company will bring significant insight into the things you really care about as an employee. What is it like to work there? Be aware that a lot of the public information is just a positive spin, so you should get the inside scoop if you can. If you cannot find someone who works in that firm to talk to, then find someone who is in the same industry and has contact with that firm. For example, a company's website may assert certain values, but what is said on that website may be very different from the perception of people who are doing business or competing with the company. Also, you need industry-specific knowledge to really understand how the business is positioned. Anyone in the industry can enlighten you. If you make the extra effort to actually talk to these people, your work will show in the interview. You will be asking informed, relevant questions and find yourself at a significant advantage.

Q7: When applying for a position in a company, sometimes the company asks for the candidate to write in or suggest the "expected salary." What is a reasonable amount for graduates and undergraduates to put on the applications?

A7: "Competitive."

Q8: Let's say I get the offer (and I'm ready to celebrate), but I am really disappointed with the salary they mentioned when they called with the offer, as it's lower than I expected. What should I do? Can I negotiate?

A8: First job? Usually you cannot negotiate. If you are fresh out of school and you have no experience, then you are lucky to get that job offer. The last thing you want to do is send a signal that all you are there for is money. What you want to say (no matter what the salary is), is that you really appreciate the offer. Focus on the job scope, and then talk about what role you would be playing. You want to send a clear signal to your boss and to the people you are working with that you are there for the learning experience, in addition to the paycheck. After your first job, then you have some bargaining power and the experience to negotiate aggressively through a head-hunter or one-on-one.

For most starting positions in a professional role with a firm or a large company, the salaries are set; they are not open to negotiation. There is industry-wide data available on websites (see the Resources section at the end of this section to check on current salary ranges for positions or industries you may in interested in). You can research whether the offer you have received is in line with market conditions. If your offer is far lower than the range for your position in that industry, then you have solid ground on which to open discussions with your potential employer. With a very small firm for which there may not be data, there may not be a very competitive market. If you feel you can improve on this offer, you should look for a different job. You certainly do not need to take a below-market salary and feel undervalued by this employer if you command a higher salary in this market.

Q9: How do companies set their salaries?

A9: Firms hiring on a regular basis – meaning that they hire a group of new-comers every year or so – will have the group starting at the same salary or something within a range based on prior experience. At those firms, salary is not negotiated on a one-on-one basis. The salaries should be based on supply and demand, and the standards of the industry. For example, at major accounting firms, consulting firms, investment banks and law firms, the firms are well aware of the market conditions and they have set their salaries competitively. At many of these large employers, the young associates tend to compare salaries and compile competitors' compensation packages to keep pressure on their employers to remain competitive. Check out their websites for detailed salary and benefits information.

Q10: Does the salary level indicate the quality of the job?

A10: It is one piece of information that shows how highly the employer values the employee. It is not everything, and it can be misleading in some cases. Salaries are impacted by the profitability of the company. They also reflect the value that the marketplace places on this position in this industry. Generally, salary is a reflection of market-based values, and higher quality generally commands a higher salary. Your starting salary, and the pay scale (rate of promotions and salary raises) over those first few years have a longer-term effect on the pay you can command as your career progresses (think in terms of compounded interest: 15% raises per year grow faster if based on a high first year salary).

However, there are significant exceptions to these market-based effects on pay, mostly associated with prestige or training opportunities. Some of the better firms actually do not pay top salary because of the high employee demand for the experience to be gained by working there. Some investment banks have found they can pay less than others because they have a premium brand name that young professionals want to get on their resume. Early jobs in medicine are notorious for relatively low pay, given the highly-skilled young doctors who want the experience there. In these markets, the financial rewards come later in the banker or doctor's career, when they command a very high salary after sacrifice in the early days.

Q11: What is a headhunter? Can I get a headhunter to help me find my first job?

A11: A headhunter is not a cannibal – at least not in the traditional use of the word. He or she is a person in the search or recruiting business, someone specialized in helping make matches in the employer/employee market. Search professionals maintain contacts and relationships with the major companies in the industry and geographic regions where the head-hunter specializes. When a match is made, the recruiter is paid about one month's salary.

Companies generally use search firms for executive positions and for positions involving a few years of experience. It's not economic to pay the search firm fees for a lower position, nor is it necessary, when new college graduates can be recruited directly from the university through the campus recruiting office. Search firms are helpful for employers who do not have such easy access to well-qualified professionals. Many professionals do not leave the job they are in until they have the new position lined up and negotiated. This is where the headhunter comes in: identifying candidates who are in positions already, but interested in making a move.

Q12: OK, so I can't use a headhunter yet. Should I cultivate relationships with them over time?

A12: Yes. Return their calls. Give them leads on candidates who might be interested in making a move within your industry. You and a couple of search professionals can be in a symbiotic relationship which results in your finding opportunities with the best pay and work in the shortest amount of time. They may offer good career advice along the way because they study and know your industry well. They can size you up and they must maintain their reputations with employers, so they only recommend a handful of candidates out of hundreds in their files for very hot job leads.

When you talk with them, be direct, clear and professional; tell them why it should be you that they recommend and not the other ninety people behind you. Convey a specific idea of the value and the skill sets that you have to offer; and most importantly give them three things you want them to remember about you. It is important to have this "top three" idea in mind when you convey your skill set to a headhunter. Headhunters have contacts everywhere – that's their business. As an intermediary between services buyers (employers) and sellers (employees), they help to keep the labor market efficient.

Q13: How do I find these search professionals or headhunters?

A13: First, they may find you if they hear about you in the market when they are looking for someone with your experience to fill a job opening. Second, you may hear about them through co-workers or classmates who use them to find a job. Third, you may have some exposure to them through your own company's or firm's recruiting process, because your company may hire new people through them. It is usually better to find them through these contacts than to cold call them based on a website or advertisement. However, if you have experience in the industry and you can check on their reputation, they may be happy to help you just based on a cold call. Send them your resume via e-mail with a follow-up call.

Q14: I just started work at my first company after graduation. One month into it, I have been offered another job which looks a lot more attractive. What should I do?

A14: You must think about the costs and benefits of the decision that you are going to make. If you leave the job that you have been in for only a .month, you will burn some bridges. The people who hired you, and who have been busy training you, will be disappointed. They will not say nice things about you if somebody calls them later and asks "how was this person as an employee?" They may like you very well, but they may say that you left the job after one month, which would be true and fair to say. If this is your first job, you are establishing that you are not reliable.

However, if the new job offer is so terrific and you have thoroughly researched just how terrific it is (i.e., you are not just going on a gut feel or leaping for a salary), you may feel it is an opportunity that will never come again in your lifetime. This is unlikely. If it's that great a fit for you, you will likely still fit there after a year or two.

Clear your head and be honest: there is no dream job, just a good assortment of interesting and at times tedious or difficult work. Is it really worth the damage you will leave? You risk making a lot of people quite angry, such as the people who wrote recommendation letters for you or made introductions for you to get the first job. You are going to annoy several people around you if you make the switch. If you still want to leap for it, you should be very frank and make sure that your current employer understands the situation and why you made the choice. Be very apologetic. Give the company that you are with plenty of time to make the right adjustments. Make a sincere apology and make sure that the space you leave behind is extremely well taken care of.

Q15: What is a reasonable number of years to work for one company? Is it better to move around or stay in one company?

A15: Different industries have different standards. For example, in the financial sector, you see quite a lot of movement in firms in investment banking, and less in other types of banking or insurance. You must be careful that you practice what is considered a norm in that industry or profession. Different countries have different customs as well. You do not want to raise alarms by following a different pattern, but you also need to make your own decisions about professional moves based on your opportunity set and goals, as well as your personal life.

There are pros and cons associated with staying with one company for a long time. The advantages of a long stay include seniority in the firm, as well as the vesting of pensions or other perks that come with climbing the ladder in that organization. The downside is that your experience is limited to one place, and you may become less flexible (or be perceived that way) by outsiders. If you move, typically you should move to a better or more attractive offer with higher pay, a promotion in terms of responsibility, and so on. We noticed that people who move every few years tend to move up the corporate ladder quite quickly, and that is one way of doing it. The other way is to stay in one company, show a great deal of loyalty and really dig a deep well there, becoming part of the institution.

I think less than two years at one job is a little bit too short. If you served over three years at a company or professional services firm, that would be considered pretty acceptable. Three to four years at one job looks fine on your resume.

Q16: What if I hate my first job and want to quit as soon as possible. Should I quit right away? How can I cope?

A16: If you really feel you somehow landed in a very narrow job and the mission of your firm and its clients is not compelling for you for some reason, then stick it out for a reasonable period of time – a year or two at least. There's no reason for you to have a three-month full time job on your resume – this will look like you got fired or you couldn't handle the job for some reason. You can handle almost anything for a year or so. You may find by the time you get nine or ten months into the job that things have really changed. You may find that the impossible jerk who was managing your first project is someone you haven't seen in months, and now you're working for people who are really showing you the ropes and letting you see the big picture.

In a large organization, the people around you are likely to change, and your projects will change, over time. Your negativity may be due to not really understanding how the firm works, feeling that you have not found a support network or that you are not a good fit within the organization. Realize that these things take time and investment on your part. Be patient and research your options by talking to your colleagues, managers, staffing coordinator, folks in other departments, etc. Make an effort to better understand your environment.

Q17: What if my school career center does not have as many job postings as other schools? Where do I find alternative sources for job openings and internships?

A17: It is a poor idea to rely on one source for your job information – especially when it is the same job office as every other student at your school – unless your career center is truly outstanding. For graduate school placement centers, you can expect significantly more help. At college graduation, cast your net wide. When you are job-hunting, let people around you know. Helpful connections may pop up where you least expect them. And be kind to the older generation who want to have you go talk to their friends or some distant relation. Even if it's not what you think is your dream connection, the older generation can have surprisingly good foresight!

You should also check all the websites that you possibly can get hold of (starting with the Resources at the end of this section) because the job information is not going to be repeatedly posted everywhere. There may be some good jobs that you really like posted in some obscure corner of the world. Typically, if the job posting goes up in your school, then you are competing with everyone in your school, whereas if your uncle tells you about the job in his company, then you may be competing with only a handful of people for that job.

Q18: How can personal contacts help me land a job?

A18: Some people find terrific jobs without going through the formal channels at their school's career center, especially if they have a good idea of what they are looking for. Personal connections can be contacts that you yourself make. They do not have to be a favor to your parents, and they do not have to be based on someone else recommending you. You can find the people you need to impress on your own.

How does this happen? You can go directly to the firm. Cut out all the middle people. Send resumes to two types of people internally at the potential employer: (i) the human resources/recruiting people (who are helpful but are not the ultimate decision makers), and (ii) the decision-makers (the senior manager of the department who is looking for help from someone like you or the hiring partner). One or the other will pick up on a good quality candidate. This can work very effectively for well-organized firms where hiring decisions are made quickly and by clear-minded senior people who know what they like when they see it. It's okay to be a little aggressive.

Don't be reactive, but proactive. For example, I once read an article in *The Asian Wall Street Journal* written by a banker regarding the Korean economy that interested me. I picked up the phone and called him. You will see that in an investment bank they will not filter you, so I was on the phone with that guy in five minutes; I said I liked his article and continued the conversation. Guess what? I ended up working in his office.

Q19: What does it mean to be proactive when I am conducting a job search?

A19: The first step is to identify what type of job you are going to search for. Once you have identified the basic industry and types of the positions that you are seeking in that industry, then you are ready to talk to some people. Obviously, your own university's career service office is the first place to check. But they may have little or nothing in your particular field. The next step is to start researching companies and to start researching alumni, people from your home town, people your parents may know, and people whom your professors may know. You start looking for any sort of contact. It may be a second- or third-degree connection that you have to a person in a certain company, certain place, or certain field. But if you can make that contact, you will learn something that will eventually lead you to the job you seek. Being proactive means that you are doing your own research – identifying what your destination is and building a connection to that place. You create opportunities for yourself. Once you have created a set of options, then you can start eliminating. But do not eliminate anything until you have generated some offers that are in the realm of acceptability to you.

Q20: How do I get someone to meet with me if they do not have a job to offer me?

A20: To get your foot in the door and actually talk to someone, you do not have to ask them for a job. It may be difficult to get any attention if you are going to ask for a job. However, you can approach them as a part of your information gathering process. You may write an alumnus of your university who is working in a nice firm in an industry you are interested in. Tell them who you are and that you are interested in working in that industry, too. Do not be shy. They will be flattered – you are implicitly complimenting them. You can ask for ten or fifteen minutes of their time to talk about their career and what is like to work in their industry. You are asking for an informational interview. This contact could lead to other contacts if the alumnus likes you and is impressed with you during a ten minute conversation. Start with the most obvious connections that you can make and spread out to build your network.

Q21: I have just received a job offer and it's an okay opportunity. However, I am waiting to hear from another company that I much prefer. What should I do?

A21: You need two approaches: one is defensive and the other is offensive. Defense: you need to make sure that this offer does not go away. Tell them you need more time to think about this and clear it through the proper channels. Offense: you need to speak to the firm you prefer and tell them that you have received an offer from a competitor. If you use those words, you will signal to them that (a) you are in high demand, and (b) you have a time constraint. Your value in the eyes of the preferred firm will rise when you let them know. Firms can move very quickly if they have the right incentives. This situation presents the right incentives.

Q22: Do some major companies have specialized job search processes? How do I find out exactly what's involved?

A22: Start with their websites, where you will usually find detailed instructions and may be required to enter your resume and application electronically before you are welcome to contact the company. If the information seems inadequate or confusing, call the recruiting/human resources contacts listed on the website and/or talk with other students who have gone through the recruiting process with this company. The following pages show some examples of the on-line recruiting process as of 2006 for large companies recruiting in the Seoul market.

Sample Recruiting Processes at Large Companies:

A. Recruiting Process for L'Oreal in Korea

- **Internship Program**
  The first step of recruiting for the company is its Internship Program.
  Eligible Applicants: Undergraduates (3rd & 4th year), Graduate Students
  Period: 2 months (Summer: July & August; Winter: January & February)
  Assignment: Interns are Given Projects, and Give a Presentation at the end of the internship
  Payment: 800,000 won per month

- **Summer Intern Schedule**
  Campus Visit: April, May (notified at the website)
  Application time: During May
  English Group Debate: First week of June
  Intern Workshop: Last week of June

- **Winter Intern Schedule**
  Campus Visit: October, November
  Application time: During November
  English Group Debate: First week of December
  Intern Workshop: Last week of December

- **Management Trainee**
  According to the result of one's performance during Internship, one will be hired as a Management Trainee.

* Details are subject to change. Please refer to the website for the confirmed schedule.

Source: www.loreal.co.kr (viewed in March 2006)

B. Recruiting Process for Proctor & Gamble in Korea

Applying

- One may apply through internship or at all times. (www.pg.co.kr/jobs/application.asp)

Submitting the form

- The application form is available at P&G homepage and you can only submit it online. (www.asp.co.kr/jobs/application.asp)

MAF Test

- When the application form is submitted, the applicant needs to take the online MAF (Management Application Form) Test.
- One will receive an ID and Password after the test.
- The ID and Password is needed to revise the application and to find out the result. A password will not be issued more than once.

Written Examination

- The date of the written examination (or the scheduled date of the examination for the internship) will be notified to those concerned through e-mail.
- If an examinee does not arrive on time, or one does not bring the necessary documents (resume and self-introduction, record of grades, copy of Toeic/Toefl, and other copies of other certificates), then one will not be allowed to take the examination. Submitted documents are to be kept by the company. Refer to the website for the examining subjects.
- The location of the written examination is at the head office. One may refer to the map on the website. The examination will take approximately two hours.
- The result will be posted after one week on the website. (It will not be notified individually through email.) Do not forget the ID and Password.

Interviews

- There will be at least three interviews, and one of them will be in English.

Source: www.pg.co.kr (viewed in March 2006)

C. Recruiting Process for Samsung Companies in Korea

- Eligible Applicants: Usually college graduates; however, no limitation in education
- Application Period: At all times according to the needs of each company.
  The Open Recruit will be posted when many new employees are needed.
- Application Process:
- **Submit Applications – Document Evaluation – SSAT – Interviews – Medical Examinations – Final Acceptance**
  - Examining Documents: To evaluate whether the applicant is competent there will be a basic evaluation according to the demands of each company. Written facts will be inspected.
  - SSAT: Tests of Basic Knowledge and Specialized Knowledge.
  - Foreign Language Skills and other Certificates are treated preferentially.
  - Interviews:

First Interview	The applicant's personality and ability to respond (interviewing time 10~20 minutes per person)
Second Interview	Presentations /group debates/ role plays according to different departments. ● Presentations Tests basic knowledge and ability to respond. (10~20 minutes per person) Specialized questions according to departments. ● Group Debates Tests professional knowledge. Comprehensive evaluation of the applicant's logic, persuasiveness, and communication skills. (40 minutes per 4 to 6 persons) ● Role Playing Applicants will be evaluated upon problem solving skills and handling given roles in each unit. (10 minutes per person)

List of Samsung Companies

Electronic Industries	Samsung Electro-mechanics, Samsung SDI, Samsung Corning, Samsung Corning Precision Glass, Samsung SDS, Samsung Networks
Machinery & Heavy Industries	Samsung Heavy Industries, Samsung Techwin
Chemical Industries	Samsung Total Petrochemicals, Samsung Petro-chemicals, Samsung Fine Chemicals, Samsung BP Chemicals
Finance Services	Samsung Life Insurance, Samsung Fire & Marine Insurance, Samsung Card, Samsung Securities, Samsung Investment Trust Management, Samsung Venture Investment
Other Affiliated Companies	Samsung Corporation, Samsung Engineering, Cheil Industries, Samsung Everland, The Shilla Hotels & Resorts, Cheil Communications, S1 Corporation, Samsung Lions, Samsung Medical Center, Samsung Human Resources Development Institute, Samsung Advanced Institute of Technology, Samsung Economics Research Institute, Samsung Foundation of Culture, Samsung Welfare Foundation, The Ho-Am Foundation, Samsung Press Foundation

- Note: If the information you provide is proven to be false, your application will be dismissed.

If any question, contact the company. (Q&As on the website)

Source: www.dearsamsung.co.kr (viewed in March 2006)

Chapter 6 Internships

Q1: During my undergraduate years, I did not have many chances to do internships. I am wondering if that will disadvantage me in trying to find a job?

A1: Doing an internship in and of itself does not get you the job. Internships do not necessarily involve doing serious work. You get your feet in the industry and you find out what's going on there. But in terms of just work *per se*, the internship experience is not necessarily time better spent than coursework or an extracurricular activity in which you excel.

What internships can do for you is to build some connections to the people and the institution where you are an intern. Getting to know some people there and maintaining contact with them after graduation is the most valuable aspect of the internship. So, not doing an internship does not really hurt your chances of getting a job.

Q2: I have an opportunity to be an intern with a government ministry, but the work there is unrelated to the type of work I want to do in the future. Should I take the unrelated internship?

A2: Doing an internship in a field in which you have little interest in working in the future will not harm you, but it comes at an opportunity cost. Your time is valuable, and you are spending it in an internship when you could be doing something related to your real interests. For students who want to get internships, I strongly recommend that they look for something in an industry or company that offers experience related to their areas of professional interest.

You can approach the area of interest both in terms of the industry and the role you play there as an intern. What you do in a specific job can be as important as which company you work for. For example, even if you are at a financial institution, you can work in marketing. This would provide you with useful experience that would be applicable if you choose to work in the marketing department of a manufacturing or industrial company in the future. In any case, analyze what you will gain from the work you do in an internship, as much as from the identity of the employer.

Q3: Are internships expected by first-job employers these days? If they seem to be expected in my home country, are they similarly expected everywhere?

A3: There seems to be a trend toward more internships these days. It's crazy. For some reason, students think that employers like people with a lot of internship experience, and for some reason employers say that they do. I say it is crazy because in many cases the internship experience does not translate into any specific skill set, or the employer would be just as happy to have someone with no internship experience as someone with the internship experience. So there is a game being played with a different impact than just the value of the internship: if you had an internship at a very prestigious place, then the employers are impressed because it means the intern beat out 200 other competitors to get that internship position. She must be good! There is a kind of signaling process going on.

If you are seeking a job with firms who we recognize as liking internship experiences, then be strategic: try to get an internship at a place that is highly competitive so that you can say "I got this internship and I had to beat 200 other applicants to get it." Do not go to any old internship, where they would accept anybody, because it is well-known that they accept just anybody. If interning at a company will not send positive signals to the future employers you really want to impress, then you should pass. Spend that time in a higher-impact activity.

Q4: What kinds of internships are good?

A4: I think that the best internships are the ones in an industry where you would like to work later, or with the particular company that you would like to work for. If you intern at a company and you do a great job, have a great attitude and get to know people there, then they will realize that having you join as one of the regular employees would be beneficial to them.

An internship is really a trial period. Employers like to see you at work for a while before they commit to hiring you – that is why they offer internships. If you can really impress your colleagues during the summer or winter vacation internship, then you have a good chance of being offered a job later on. I think those are the best internships.

The other kind of internship that you should seek is one that allows you to learn a lot. Even if it is a position with a no-name company or some odd organization, if you can go in there and feel that you have a lot to learn, then it can be a very beneficial experience. Later, when seeking a job, you can use that type of internship experience as a platform for talking about your experiences there. The actual work you did may impress future employers.

Q5: How do I decide which internship and first job to try for?

A5: Think about two things: (i) the value of the experience to you in the future, and (ii) what the item signals when it is added to your resume.

Whether you are applying to internships, jobs, or graduate schools it is important to remember that whatever you put on your resume sends a quality signal. It not only offers information about who you are and what you have done, but it signals the quality standards you hold for yourself, personally and professionally. Unfortunately, you must compete with many other applicants for the most prestigious jobs and positions. The person making the decision is going to make an initial cut based on what is on the resume. The resume items serve as signals – as proxy information for who you really are. So when you are getting the internship or job, you should get the best one you can get.

Q6: How do internships help with first jobs and future employment prospects?

A6: Internships helped me tremendously upon graduating from college. The first internship that I had was with a government regulatory agency, and that really helped me to get to my second internship with a prestigious firm – which then helped me to get my first full time job with another top-tier firm. For me, it developed like a pyramid. You will find that companies in the same industry or geographic location value the experience you have at competitors and other firms with a high-quality reputation.

Q7: What is the end-game in the pyramid? How do I know where to start building this type of internship and job structure?

A7: It is difficult to know when you are 18 or 19 years old what you will be doing and what you want to be doing for the rest of your life until you retire in your 50's or 60's. Someone told me this: in your twenties, you should try everything that you have a passion for. In your thirties, of the many things you have a passion for and you have tried, choose one (generally people do not have one and only one passion, they have many passions: some lawyers love art, others may love fashion…). Choosing one does not mean it is the only one forever, but it is the one at the time, given your experience, given your view and your situation and it is the one that you will try at that time.

Then you focus during your thirties. By the time you reach your forties, you will be a specialist or an expert in that area. You might become a partner or managing director at that point, and in your fifties you can become a sort of rain-maker ("business development" role – in charge of client relationships). In your undergraduate years, the mission is to build the broad foundation of this life-long pyramid of experience. Your internship opportunities both add to the foundation and help inform you as to which direction you will choose for the next layer.

Q8: How do I apply for an internship? How do I start the process and introduce myself?

A8: Start by writing a cover letter and sending it, together with your resume, to the organization(s) where you are interested in getting an internship. The cover letter should be brief and basic, covering just four main points: 1) self introduction ("I am an economics major at Big State University…"), 2) expression of why the internship is a good fit for your career plans, 3) explanation of how and why you are qualified to perform well in the internship with this company ("I am uniquely qualified to be a Mount Everest guide due to my experience climbing the peak last summer and my ability to speak fluent Nepali···), and 4) information for how to contact you and a promise that you will be contacting them in the near future. Then you have to do it – schedule when you will make that phone call on the day you mail the letter! See a sample cover letter in the box below.

Cover Letter Example – Seeking an Internship

Sally Student
987 My Street
Campus 12345

March 1, 2006

Ms. Manager
BigCo, Inc.
P.O. Box 1234
567 BigCo Blvd.
Out There, Asia 10987

Dear Ms. Manager:

I am interested in a Summer Management Training Internship with BigCo, Inc. I learned about your summer internship program from an article in *The Asia Times* on February 29, 2006. This opportunity interests me because I have the professional and educational background necessary to make positive contributions to your firm.

I intend to pursue a career in management in a high-tech industry such as BigCo's after completing my degree in International Studies, with a concentration in Business, in 2007. My studies in management, finance and economics have a global perspective. This has prepared me well to make valuable contributions to your company's operations, both at home in Korea and globally. Through my varied courses, which are described in my resume, I have developed the ability to learn new skills quickly and independently, and to interact effectively in a business environment. I would look forward to applying all these abilities at BigCo, Inc.

As a student leader, I have applied my management skills when I co-chaired the university-wide Graduation Ceremony and Student Fund-Raising Efforts for Tsunami Victims in Winter 2005, where we raised 10 billion won in aid money. My coursework has also provided me opportunities to develop practical finance skills: in Fall 2005, my team won the "Capital Funding Challenge" with our entrepreneurial business plan for a manufacturing business. My resume (enclosed) details these and other experiences.

I would appreciate the chance to interview with you at your earliest convenience. If you have questions or would like additional information, contact me at (123) 456-7890 any Tuesday or Thursday after 10 a.m., or e-mail me at sallystudent@email.com. Thank you for your time.

Sincerely,

Sally Student

Enclosure: Resume

Chapter 7 The Resume

Q1: What kind of resume looks good?

A1: A professional one that shows you are qualified and worth bringing in for an interview. Save the pink paper and perfume for another occasion; your resume should be professional in content and style. It should reflect your experience and be interesting (without the flowers or glitter glue). A good resume tells the reader a lot of interesting facts about the person. It must cover the basics: education, work and other relevant experience, achievements and awards. Follow a standard format and make it readable with some white space on the page. Use correct grammar and bullet points, and include dates and cities where you did your training and activities. Show as much geographic diversity as possible.

Your resume fits on one page. You are far too young to have a two-page resume. At the bottom include an Other Activities section that is brief. Here you can include some cool stuff you have done, like playing Annie in the Broadway musical, teaching scuba diving or finishing the Ironman triathlon, or playing guitar with Franz Ferdinand. Maybe you run a soup kitchen for homeless people at your place of worship? Your Other Activities can convey something special about you – your attitude, some accomplishments and your passions. But be sure you can really do all you claim – your boss may just ask you to prove your professed tennis expertise! That's what will interest the reader. In general, the resume should be very professional, just like everything about the interviewing student candidate.

Q2: What is my resume used for?

A2: It gets you the interview. It gets you in the door, based on your qualifications. It also serves as the basis for the discussion you will have in your interview. The people interviewing you will be reading it and asking you to talk about the experiences you list there. They may be reading it for the first time. They have only 20-30 minutes to think about you, and they will prefer to hear what you have to say in person rather than spending much time looking at what you put in writing on the resume.

At the firm, your resume provides the information that gets culled in the human resources/recruiting office. If the resume shows you meet the requirements for the position, then you get called for the interview. If not, you either get no response at all or you get a polite and brief rejection letter: "Dear Ms. X, Thank you for your interest in our company··· we will keep your resume on file··· best of luck··· don't call us, we'll call you." Accept these with humor. My roommate in college took to posting her dozens of rejection letters on the door to our room at the dormitory. It made everyone laugh to see how many polite and strange ways there are to say "no job for you." It also reminded us as we went through the stressful job search process that we all get rejected a few times before we find our professional home – well, most people do, anyway. It's nothing to fear, nothing to hide, just a process.

Q3: Do I use the same resume for every employer or position?

A3: No. Resumes can be tailored to the employer, both in format and content. A student who is applying for a job with Amnesty International should highlight his civil society or other advocacy work, political activities and the like. Certainly, mention related course work, publications or research. A student applying for a finance job should highlight her honors or awards in finance, math, economics or business internships and other relevant experience. Relevant information is better than irrelevant information, and should be more fully described. The format of a resume should be consistent with what you find in your standard resume guidebooks. There is some choice to make about what order to list the sections and where to add detail, based on what you want to highlight.

Q4: If I worked at the ABC Company for only three months, do I need to put it on my resume for the future?

A4: You choose what to put on your resume. Everything that you put on your resume must be true. However, you do not have to tell everything about yourself on your resume. I believe that if there is a significant gap in time and you spent that time in prison, you will be asked about where you spent that time and you must answer truthfully. For a three month job, if the job was good and you have interesting things to share in an interview about your experiences on that job, by all means put it down and give that job a good description. If the job does not contribute to your case that you are qualified for a professional career in the field you are now interested in, you may want to omit it. For example, some time spent mowing lawns, delivering newspapers, waiting tables or life guarding may not help your story when you go interview with a human rights organization.

However, your volunteer work with domestic violence victims would be a must-include item, even if you were only involved for a short period of time.

Q5: I have some holes in my resume – some periods of time when I took some time off from school and work and I just traveled. I also had a break from school for family reasons when my parent was ill. How do I describe these matters on my resume? It was a one-year period, then several weeks. Should I just leave that time blank?

A5: It's not a good idea to have a very big blank. If there are specific activities that you undertook – for example, nursing your grandmother – it is worth providing this information in brief format. On the other hand, if it is a short period of time like several weeks or a few months, then it is perfectly okay to leave that blank.

In the interview, you may be asked some questions about anything you write down on the resume, including time spent on non-traditional activities. In fact, you can expect to be asked about the more unique items on your resume and serious time off may be at the top of the list. You should be willing to be very specific. For example, you need to make a good case for why what you did deserved your devoting a full year to it. For any special activities you have undertaken outside of study and work, think about how those activities have contributed to your development and personal growth, as well as contributing to your professional talents.

Q6: Do I need to include everything in my resume? What if I am not particularly proud of certain things?

A6: You need not confess all your sins on your resume. However, at this tender age, most everything you have done constitutes a valuable, formative experience for you and there is probably very little you really need to exclude. If it involves time "off," think a lot about what you gained from this in a positive manner: is it fair to think of it not as time off, but as time pursuing a special dream or rising to the challenge at a time of need for your family? Do not describe travel time or other non-study periods in frivolous terms, both for the impression it will leave with your employer and for the sake of your own mental health.

Going into the interview process, you need to get your life experience – all of it – sorted out so that you can tell your story with confidence. It is critical that you inspire confidence in the people you are applying to work with and for. If you have feelings of regret or disappointment, do not spill your concerns out to a potential new colleague in an interview or otherwise. They have not invited you to hear about your psychological baggage, they are interested in hiring you to make a positive contribution to their enterprise. There is rarely a sympathy offer in the workplace, and you do not need to ask for it. Reflect on the long-term value of your non-traditional use of time and position it in the context of your resume so it supports your big picture and current goals.

Q7: I'm a senior now and I'm looking back on my university years. Academics were important for me, but I also put a lot of focus on various extracurricular activities. How much will these activities help me in the job market?

A7: Extracurricular activities can be very important. Their value depends on the quality of effort you invested, and your accomplishments. If you saved the world, surely, that's going to count for a lot more than if you had internships at the usual destinations. Either of those will be more valuable than if you were a member of many organizations, but not an officer or a leader at any of them. If you founded a company or did something very entrepreneurial, involving leadership skills and running a large organization, these activities speak very well about you as a person and about your leadership abilities, experience and potential. It is good if you can demonstrate your ability to apply yourself successfully in different situations. In general, when I interview or look at applications, I think a candidate's activities are an important, relevant source of information about the candidate.

Q8: In which activities should I get involved for purposes of building an impressive resume?

A8: None. You should get involved in things you care about so you will have an interesting and productive life. But if you are a senior and you feel you have little "official" activity of resume quality, then, by all means, get involved in something. Do consider that your time should be well spent on a personal level, as well as for its professional impact. Write a thesis and join a political action committee.

For the most part, resumes tend to look pretty much the same. You have entered a good university, you have gotten a good GPA, and you have worked at some internships. These are the quality basics, and you must include them. But where are you going to make a difference? Your key difference will come in the other areas that you undertook voluntarily. Maybe you went up Mt. Everest with a blind person on your back. Or you ran seven marathons in one week or something like that. If you have not done those things, then do them and convey the important information so it gets noticed. I think belonging to the YMCA or a lot of student circles is not very important unless that group managed to kick out the president from her office or educated underprivileged children or something like that. You should be doing something that is an eye-opener. You want the interviewer to say "Wow! I must ask this person some follow up questions." Those are the best kinds of extracurricular activities.

Q9: Should I put all my many extracurricular activities on the resume?

A9: Only if the activities send a positive signal about you. Include anything you did intensively, anything for which you won an award or received some sort of recognition. Maybe you went to a big national convention? Any worthwhile project can say a lot about you. Joining lots of clubs to have a dozen things listed on the resume is a bad idea for the resume, as well as a waste of your valuable time. If you did join a dozen clubs, I would not put them all on the resume because it just looks like you are trying to fill the white space on the paper – that you are over-committed and did not take one thing seriously or do one thing well. Study, learn a lot and do one or two things well.

Q10: Where do I send my resume?

A10: You send it to the human resources manager. You may want to specify what area or position you are interested in. Let us say you are applying to a bank and you would like to be a research analyst, or you are applying to a fund management company and you would like to be a junior fund manager or a trader. It is not a bad idea to say what department in that company interests you. Before doing so, you should study the company and the industry so you are personally informed and your resume is recognized as an applicant from a person interested in x area. You should not leave it up to the recruiting staff to decide which type of job is right for you – they are equipped to look for certain factors and arrange interviews, but they are not your personal career advisers, and they are not the decision-makers for the company's ultimate hiring decisions for professional positions in most cases.

Q11: Is there a certain correct format for my resume? Where do I begin to get my presentation looking right?

A11: Generally, your name should be large and prominent at the top of the resume – this is all about you. Your contact information goes right below your name, and it's got to be correct. Obviously, you need to be reachable at the numbers/address you provide; send out a new resume if your mom finally kicks you out and your contact info changes. Beyond that, arrange your information from most important to least, identifying time periods and locations. Leave some white space and keep it readable. Use active voice and a consistent style. One example is provided for you on the following page; see the resume writing guides in Resources at the end of this volume for many more examples. You will find that format varies just a little. Your goal is communication, so legibility and presentation are the keys. There is otherwise no "right" or "wrong" format (except were the employer requires your information to be in their prescribed format).

Gina Graduate

SCHOOL
999 University Drive
Blossom, Asiana 44444
(000) 111-2222
ginag@iu.edu

HOME (after June 2006)
1234 W. Home Ave
Hong Kong 123456
085-321-1234
gina85@yahoo.com

OBJECTIVE

Position in financial research, leading to management in corporate finance.

EDUCATION

Asiana University

Bachelor of Arts in History, with a Minor in Finance and Economics, expected June 2006

Grade Point Average: 3.88 out of possible 4.0

Emphasis: Modern China

Minor: Finance and Economics

Honors: Senior Honor Society, Business Plan Contest honorable mention

Senior Thesis: "China's 21st Century Challenge: Reform in Financial Institutions"

INTERNSHIP EXPERIENCE

First Bank, Inc., Blossom, Asiana, 2005

Research Assistant, Summer and Fall Semesters

Assisted manager of corporate finance; wrote and edited the bank's Investor Relations website.

LANGUAGE AND COMPUTER SKILLS

Native Asiana, Fluent English (TOEFL XXX), Conversational Chinese and Chinese Characters

Microsoft Word, Excel, PowerPoint

REFERENCES

Available upon request from Professor O. Archive of Asiana University (senior thesis advisor), Professor D. Numbers of Asiana University (Finance Department), and Ms. Rela Shuns, Manager of Corporate Finance at First Bank, Inc.

Chapter 8 Recommendation Letters, Transcripts and Grades

Q1: In applying for summer internships, should I offer to supply a letter of recommendation? Would that actually help my chances?

A1: It is always better to provide a recommendation letter. Even if the firms do not specifically ask to see your recommendations, it does not hurt you to send them, especially if they say good things about you. Some resumes note that "Recommendation letters are available upon request." If you are going to include this notation on your resume, it is a good idea to write whose recommendation would be available upon request. You are likely only to have a couple of recommendations, so it is not too much information to add to your resume.

Q2: If I am looking for a job overseas, are letters of recommendation important?

A2: For people who are looking to move to a global market where the employer is not that familiar with your former work experience or the quality of your educational institution, letters of recommendations are even more important. They may be required. Originals, or letters in signed and sealed envelopes, may even be needed.

If you were moving from a position in a local company to a

position in another local company, the second employer would be pretty familiar with the quality of that first employer. The new employer likely would understand what your job title meant at that first employer, and would be familiar with the ranking of your university. But when you go abroad, letters of recommendation (in English or the local language) would be even more important because the quality of the institution and the quality of your experience would be less familiar to the potential employer in the foreign market.

You should keep your letters of recommendation in a file over your lifetime – even if you think you have retired at some point, or are changing industries or types of career. Every time you work in an internship, or if you are leaving a job after only a year or two in the position and moving on to a better job, you should ask your immediate supervisor and a senior person at the firm you are leaving to send you off with a letter for your file. Ask anyone there with whom you had a good relationship, and don't be shy – they will be complimented that you value their opinion and their recommendation. You should ask them before you leave, and get the signed letter before you leave. It is much more work to call them months or years later and have to worry about whether they remember you, or what lasting impression your work left after you were gone. It is even difficult to locate people you once worked with, as they change positions and employers as often as you. Your former employer may even cease to exist if it gets bought by another firm.

Letters you request at the end of an internship, research project or job may be addressed "to whom it may concern" if you do not have an immediate use for them. Keep them – they can serve you well for the rest of your career, whatever direction it make take. Some of the most valuable things that can be said about a person in a letter of recommendation have to do with the character of the employee ("trustworthy," "careful," "always met a deadline," "diligent," "good team player," "effective leader," "entrepreneurial," "problem-solver") and not with traits specific to the position or the industry.

Q3: If I'm applying for a job abroad, how can I educate my potential employers about the high quality of my university?

A3: When you provide your grade information, you can also provide some very brief information about where your university ranks within your home country. More helpful might be some objective information comparing your university to other universities in the place where you're applying for the job. You don't want to attach too much information, but a little bit of something indicating the very high quality of your university in terms that the foreign employer can understand may help the perception of your grades and may put your transcript into proper context for the employer. The employer is unlikely to research your school independently. You have to sell yourself and the quality of your education to them. In a job search process, just put something in your cover letter. The cover letter is going to be sweet and simple, and there you can note two or three things about your school: e.g., Ewha Womans University is the largest women's university in the world; its international studies program is top-ranked in Korea, etc.

Chapter 9 The Interview

Q1: What is the purpose of the interview? What are they trying to learn by meeting me for just a few minutes?

A1: The interview is a face-to-face meeting with people at the company. A first-round interview may be with the recruiter or it may be on campus. It is usually with one person from the employer. The second round interview is a call-back where you meet with more people. Some companies have many rounds, some just one or two. They are looking for whether you would fit well with the general culture of the company. They are trying to gauge your level of interest in the company and evaluating your communication abilities. Impressing on them that you are smart, confident, well-prepared and keenly interested in their company is the key to getting the job offer.

The company is not looking for someone who can add immediate value. Even with a new hire who was a business major, that person is not going to add much value to the firm. Statistically (on average), they will not add value until their second or third year with the company. Many interviews are conducted by junior staff who will be your immediate seniors and these people are asking themselves whether you are a person who will contribute to their team, and whether they want to spend long hours working with you. The interviewer may also be checking on the veracity of your resume.

Q2: What are some examples of questions I should expect in a standard interview?

A2: Anything and everything from your resume, especially the more interesting bits. What are your strengths and weaknesses? (Make them sound somewhat relevant to the job···) Describe a time you mastered a great challenge in your life. (Try to keep it professional···) How do you see yourself in five years? Ten years? (You should talk about yourself in a professional role in this field, not about what you would be wearing, or who you plan to be dating then···) How will you decide which firm to join? Who else are you interviewing with? Do you plan to go to graduate school at some point?

Q3: Do companies in some industries have tests or special skills they are trying to detect in the interview process?

A3: Financial institutions (such as investment banks) will want to see if you can handle finance issues and work with numbers. Management consulting firms throw business and logic problems at you verbally and see how your mind works as you think through a brand-new problem in real time. Stock brokerage firms may see how you do cold-calling clients. A sales position interview may require you to prove you can sell. Management trainee programs will be looking for your communication abilities, especially spoken communication. A newspaper will ask to see samples of your written work. It is critical that you research the interview method before you go in, so you know what to expect in addition to the standard questions about things you list on your resume and your best and worst life experiences.

Q4: What is the best strategy for dealing with an interview question, if I don't know the answer to that question?

A4: Let me tell you the worst strategy: just saying nothing is the worst strategy. I think a good way to answer a question when you do not have much information is to be honest and say that this is something that you know very little about. Do not try to pretend you know something you do not: you will probably be found out, and why would they hire a liar? Be frank if you do not know the answer, but do not just leave it there.

You are there to show why you should be hired to solve problems for this employer. They most likely are less concerned about whether you already know the answer, but are more interested in how you would find the answer if you needed to find the answer for a work-related problem. Think of this as your first assignment, and tell your interviewer how you would go about analyzing it or how you would approach that question. You may not be giving the full answer (the conclusion), but at least you are outlining how you would think through the problem.

Q5: What do I wear to an interview?

A5: Your interview is your prime opportunity to show that you will fit well into this organization. You should dress as if you belong at the firm, in the role for which you are applying. This means you will wear what the other professionals wear at this company.

Everything you say and do, including your personal appearance and your behavior should reflect that you belong at this company. Some industries are very easy to predict. Business formal is the norm in most major cities. If you are not sure, you can ask the person who is setting up your interview (usually the human resources department or recruiter, or an administrative assistant in that function). If you are still unsure for some reason, err on the conservative side and wear a suit and tie for men, suit for women – not too sexy, not too stiff.

Q6: What is business formal attire?

A6: For men, it is a suit and a tie. "Suit" means matching fabric in the jacket and pants. If you buy one thing in the year you are interviewing for a job, buy one good quality suit and white professional shirt. Women, save the lacy tank top and strappy sandals for another occasion. No rhinestones, no prints. Your dressing goal is to look professional. Your clothes should not be particularly memorable, as you want the memory to be of your sparkling personality, sharp mind and keen attitude. Invest in one reasonably nice dark suit for your interview and make it a relatively conservative one. You can get splashy later, after you have got the job and have proven you are wise enough to know the limits of good taste.

Q7: Someone asked me if I would like to go for lunch or dinner as a part of the interview. Should I accept?

A7: Yes, you are expected to join the lunch or dinner if you are invited as part of the interview. Declining shows a lack of interest or fear. The meal is the key opportunity for the interviewers – usually junior staff who are sizing you up – to see how you act in a less formal setting. If they give you the thumbs up, they are conveying that they are willing to work with you and your chances of getting the offer are much better. If they give you the thumbs down, then you have missed your shot and the chance will not come again. This is why you interview with many firms, not just one!

Q8: *OK, I'm at the lunch or dinner with the company people. How do I act?*

A8: Be yourself. Go with the professional side of yourself today, not the wild and crazy party person on this particular occasion. No matter how casual they act, always try to err on the side of being professional and at least somewhat reserved if you are the open, gregarious sort. "Be yourself" means playing the professional role for which you may be hired: imagine the person you will be in this job, and behave as you would like to see yourself behaving in the professional role. This does not mean being stiff or fake, it means being the person you want to become.

The company people are using this time to see the person behind the resume. They are taking up a whole lunch hour to spend with you, and you must not waste their time. None of you is there for the food, you have objectives to fulfill. For example, you should think of the top three things you want to convey to the employer about yourself. During the lunch, make sure that somehow you fit in those three things. There may be certain impressions of you, or questions you have about the company. Consider this practice for the many business-purpose lunches you will have in the job later on.

Q9: *Should I order drinks over lunch or dinner?*

A9: No. You are the guest here. Your hosts will order the drinks. If they order individually, you may follow suit. If there is drinking and you do join in, take it easy on the wine or whatever it is they are drinking. Participate, but drink less than they do. You are here to get an offer, not to get drunk. You can go out and celebrate after you have the offer in hand. Your interview is not over yet. You may even be called back for additional interviews in the company's office after lunch with more senior people.

Q10: What are some examples of inappropriate behavior – things I should avoid – in an interview?

A10: Anything unprofessional. Put yourself in the interviewer's shoes: would you hire a candidate in a competitive job market if they: (i) said nasty things about other people they have worked for in the past? What will they say about you in the future? (ii) have a negative attitude about anything – work, school, conditions, the weather; (iii) talk about irrelevant matters life the weather, a TV show, whether you have a pet – after all, you are both here to make important decisions about who will be hired, and you have plenty to cover without getting side-tracked; (iv) make comments that may be offensive to the interviewer, such as politics, religion, or personal choices – why risk it? You are here about the job, not the up-coming election; (v) ask about the perks or benefits instead of the work and the company? A candidate needs to convey that he or she is here to make a contribution to the business.

Q11: Female students report they often receive very personal questions in interviews based on their current status or future plans for family: marriage plans or status, plans to have children, current dependents (children, parents or others), even who they live with and whether they plan to quit work after marriage or children. What's the appropriate way to handle these questions?

A11: These personal questions are inappropriate in interviews and should be irrelevant to hiring decisions. They are illegal in many places, but we are told that in some Asian countries anti-discrimination laws relevant to this situation generally are not enforced. While you may theoretically have the right to register a complaint against the interviewer, this is not a response that is likely to get you the job.

If it is the job you are after, in spite of perhaps indelicate or illegal questions from this interviewer, you can answer without answering: say something like "marriage is something that I have not given much thought to; as you know, I have just graduated and my focus is on my career." You can respond lightly with a joke about your mom or dad wanting to find out the same thing. Frankly, anything beyond that is not their business. It is your business, though, to find out whether this firm has a bad habit of not promoting people with a certain personal life profile, or not providing on-sight child-care or leave for dependent care, etc.

Legal or not, the companies are asking these questions because they want to know whether you have outside commitments that will interfere with your working hours, loyalties, availability to travel, etc. (We are giving them the benefit of the doubt here; possibly, they are just being nosy.) In any event, you should be asking yourself the same questions as you prepare for your job search: how will you react in your professional life to the "life events" occurring in your personal life? This self-assessment is important for every person to make, male or female, and the earlier you consider how you will plan for your family life, the better prepared you will be to make decisions if and when work-family conflicts arise. You may also chart your career path in a direction that better suits you if you consider how family will impact you over time: Are you willing to travel? Do you have a support network in the city where you will live?

Does your prospective spouse have a career and an attitude about your work that is compatible with your chosen career path?

While you should engage in your own self-assessment, you by no means owe an interviewer the map to your life. Nor can you be sure how you will feel or what personal circumstances may impact you in the future. For purposes of your first-job interview, you can give a minimal answer at this point: "no current plans," or if you have current plans, then just tell them the basics if you care to share them.

One way to respond is to turn the tables on these questions, since the interviewer brought it up. You could respond for example by answering that you are not able to predict the future on those big questions yet, but since he/she brought it up, what are the company's policies in these areas? How does the company support its employees with children? Do they have on-site childcare facilities? Where do the employees' children go to school and after-school programs? What is the leave policy for paternity and maternity and for eldercare? Do many people telecommute from home?

Also, since the interviewer opened this door, you could ask how the company uses that information in its hiring decisions. Do they hire only unmarried men or only women with families? If you are planning to marry or start a family in the very near future, it may well be worth the risk to ask these questions because you really need to know. Ask about the professionals at the company: Are most of them family people? Do most of them have spouses or families? This will give you valuable insight into what kind of personal life the workplace tends to lead to. There are firms where the vast majority of people are divorced or single because they have little time outside of work to maintain their family lives. Granted, this is not the best conversation to be having during your short interview time. If possible, it is better to find out less directly about the personal lives of the employees of this firm.

For most people, to handle these intrusive personal questions, the best prospect is to find a way to answer the question very briefly and steer the conversation back to relevant topics such as your educational background. You can ask some questions about the company – about its business – to get back to relevant topics.

Q12: How about the question "who do you live with"?

A12: You can say, "is there a wrong answer to that question?" (Really, is there?) General guide: telling the truth is usually a good idea, whatever the question. This is your future full-time employer you are talking to, and whatever their value system or hiring criteria may be, you can not really win by lying now and hiding for the next few years. If they do not like you because you live with your grandmother and help take care of your niece on the weekend, is this really a place you want to work? On the other hand, this is just an employer and you are a private person, entitled to a private life, so long as your activities do not hurt the employer, negatively impact your job performance or reflect poorly on the organization. Therefore, your full disclosure of your private life is not required. In fact, it is probably not that interesting to the employer anyway! They just want to know if you have big events coming up that will impact your job, like whether you are currently pregnant.

Q13: How do I know whether to take a job with a company that asks these kinds of questions?

A13: When you are in the interview being asked a series of personal questions, it is important for you to be honest with yourself and for you to evaluate this employment opportunity. If you get the offer, you have to ask yourself whether this is the place where you want to work. Will you be miserable here because something about the job or the people you are working with is incompatible with the other things that are important in your life? You should go for jobs with companies (and seek out colleagues) who are high quality. Your professional life should be compatible with your personal life, and visa versa. That is the recipe for job satisfaction. If you are deeply unhappy at work, you may leave shortly – not a good result for you or the company.

Q14: Should I not take a job opportunity if I get the feeling the people at the employer are not supportive of family life and I eventually want to have a family?

A14: You are considering a first job commitment to this first employer, nothing more. Look at your time horizon. Also, consider the chances that pressures on this employer to be more family friendly may help the situation, for example, as its workforce matures. You do not have to solve the whole equation about family life and work when you take the first job unless the issue is already there (i.e., you already have dependents and need to care for them), or it is coming up in the near future. Look at the reports that come out about companies and their policies: if family-friendly policies are relevant to your current job search, go after jobs at companies with programs and reputations that fit your current needs. You will be happier when your whole life, personal and professional, fit together in a rational way.

It is not true that men or women who take care of children or the elderly must abandon their professional careers or their families. Flex-time schedules, work from home via the Internet and computer connections, other types of technology, and employer-supported dependent care programs have developed to enable individuals to continue work through periods of family need. Good employers now invest in supporting employees through these issues, and have experienced a high degree of employee loyalty as a result. Of course, the resources and choices available to employees differ by market, industry, geography, and according to employee position within the company. Part-time or flexible schedules may be something an employee has to earn through years of service.

Chapter 10 Professional Environment

Q1: What's different about the workplace in comparison to the university campus? Shouldn't I just be myself, wherever I am?

A1: There is a transformation that must occur right around your university graduation, from student to professional. It usually happens without a glitch for those who have landed jobs and are excited to buy a decent suit and get out in the real world. For those who fear the grown-up world or for some reason try to avoid the fact that they are about to graduate, the process can be a bit rough. Newsflash: it happens, whether you like it or not. Going to graduate school just delays the transformation due date a bit. The successful transformation affects the appearance of the graduate, her resume, the way she behaves in social situations, and hopefully her level of confidence and earning power. The graduate has accomplished a great deal and is now ready for some real-world adventures. That is both exciting and empowering. Enjoy it! And think about whether your body-piercings are something you really want to show off on the first day of the new job···You are looking to establish come credibility, right?

Q2: How should I dress on my first day at work?

A2: Like you did for the interview – like other people in the role you are going to play at work. Of course, it depends on which industry you are in. You should look at people who work there and dress accordingly. If in doubt, ask the human resources person.

Some companies have a strict dress code, such as business formal (white shirts, no silly socks, easy on the jewelry, tame colors for suits). For example, if you are working on Wall Street in New York, go with pinstripes or black for women. Brown suits are usually a bad idea, and save the linen for the Easter picnic. Business is about business, so look the part on your first day of work. Look at people who are working at that firm and take cues from people who are well-respected and successful there. If the CEO is wearing very conservative business attire, so should you. If the firm is a creative outfit like an advertising agency, a lot more artistic or colorful dress may be the expectation and the norm. And the tattoo may be a fine accessory.

Q3: I am starting a new job with a big company. People in different departments seem to dress in different ways. What images do I send by the way I dress?

A3: If you are going to work in a professional position, dress your part. If you dress like a waiter, someone will ask you to bring them a drink. Typically, business formal is expected unless the business has an explicit dress code for business casual. Some companies in some places have a business casual dress code for Fridays or summers, and there are some business environments where business casual has been put into company policy in order to create casual atmosphere, like Southwest Airlines in

Texas, some high-tech firms in Silicon Valley and on various tax-haven islands in the South Pacific. Some of these places promise to cut off any neckties worn by accident, and it's all khaki pants and polo shirts. There's even a rumor about Hawaiian shirts required to be worn at a certain tropical university….

You can easily find out by asking someone in the recruiting department who is arranging your first day or who set up your interview. Even senior executives, when they are meeting with clients, will ask about appropriate dress. If you are not sure, it is always safer to go for a conservative look.

Q4: Is it okay to check my personal e-mail from my work computer, and/or to give my work e-mail to my friends and family?

A4: One word when it comes to work e-mail: "subpoena." This is what the prosecutors and government investigators do (via a court order) if your employer ever gets investigated for anything remotely serious or potentially serious, or even if an unhappy former employee or competitor brings a lawsuit. You do not need to worry about whether your employer is obeying the law in every way. You do not know, and you cannot monitor the company or prevent the lawsuit or prosecution. You need only ask yourself the following question before you hit "send" on any e-mail you write from work (or using your work e-mail address): "how will this look as an exhibit in a trial, blown up to large poster-size print in the court case?" And "how will the journalists use this in a story about me or my employer?" E-mail is not private, and it never really gets deleted. Paper can be shredded and conversations can be kept more private if they occur in a confidential setting (or forgotten). E-mail is like a snake – don't let it bite you. Also, when you reply to the all-office e-mail announcement with an RSVP or a snide comment to your friend down the hall, don't hit "reply to all"! Just reply to the sender – no one else really wants to know if you will be attending the training seminar on Thursday.

Q5: Speaking of confidentiality, how much of the information I hear and see at work is confidential? I can talk about my job outside of work, right?

A5: You may talk about work specifics to your manager and the people on your project team at work – not everyone at work, just the people you are working directly with. What if you make your boss look bad to her boss? Why go and do that?

You can talk about some general things at work to your close friends and family – like what your company does in fairly general terms ("we are a global service leader with offices in 20 countries").

Depending on the type of company you work for, you may be restricted in what the company allows to be discussed outside the office. Firms with valuable secrets are highly sensitive to leaked information, and they will give you detailed information about what you cannot copy, remove, discuss in public, etc. All employers want to control their public image, and you are well advised not to talk to reporters or anyone who may print or quote what you say without explicit permission of the company – this is the job of the Public Relations department, not your job unless you are the PR department. Do yourself a favor and do not be the source of negative information about your company, your manager, your clients or anybody in the office. If they trace the source to you, it cannot be good for your relations or your career.

Of course it's quite a different issue if you decide you need to expose serious wrong-doing at your organization. In that case, you make a conscious decision to go public with something illegal – this is a calculated risk based on ethics or law, not a careless one based on gossip.

Q6: But I love my work and I want to brag about it to other people who may not understand how important I am. What are the consequences of just a little scoop spread around here and there to polish my image?

A6: If the information is about your company and it is not widely-known (i.e., if it is really interesting), then it is probably up to your employer when and where to make it public. Elevators, bars and hallways are notorious places for young employees to get themselves into trouble with their indiscretions. You may let off steam with your teammates who are also sworn to secrecy. Even though it is not as fun, it is a lot safer to talk shop with them. If you are talking, do it in a private environment.

Be careful out there. Information is like a disease: once it spreads, you can not control it, and you do not want to be the source or the carrier. Laws differ among nations, but the general principle (vigorously enforced in some places) is that you cannot disclose client information without risking a full-course menu of legal and practical problems for yourself, ranging from simple job loss to jail time. Unless, of course, your company has an agreement with its clients to advertise certain things about the client: then let your employer do the talking and you just nod your head and smile.

To put it simply, no good can come from your talking about work specifics, or dropping names of the cool things going at work. Enjoy your time away from work by not talking about work except in the most general terms. Your mom and your brother-in-law will be plenty impressed with you given enough time. Your employer will give you greater responsibilities if you prove yourself trustworthy in keeping confidential information. Discretion is a sign of maturity. If you prove you can keep secrets, you will become privy to many more of them.

Q7: Are people in business completely focused on earning money? How will I get along in an environment where business people haven't studied other, more important things?

A7: So you were an art history major? Or studied philosophy? Do not buy into the excuse (perhaps proposed by an unemployed friend···) that you are "selling out" if you have a respectable first job. As for your new colleagues at the firm, do not be so naive as to think that everyone in business got there with an accounting major (not that there is anything wrong with that). Even a finance major may have also studied music or world religions and chosen a career in business for practical reasons.

You may find your new colleagues and clients are far more interesting than your question pre-supposes. Talk with them. Many a law student has come back from interviewing at a Wall Street firm and reported that their interview with the senior guy was all about Russian poetry and the year they spent in the Baltics – i.e., the more interesting items on the student's resume, in which the senior guy took an interest. Turns out people in business tend to travel and have the means to contribute to arts and education at some point in their careers. The ones in their 40's and 50's have had many years to cultivate their knowledge of history, politics, the fine arts, humanities, sports, etc. – many more than you.

When you talk with people in business, you will find that they are interested in many other things as well. Like you, they mostly see making money as a means to more important ends. Everyone in a business environment brings their particular educational and professional experience to the project, and backgrounds vary widely. You may find the business managers in your firm are far from the homogenous group you imagine. If you seek them out, they may teach you to see things from a different perspective, just as your education has done.

Q8: What is it like to work in a company selling products or services? What does a day's work involve? I really can't picture life outside of an academic environment, since I've always been in school!

A8: An alumni of Ewha Graduate School of International Studies was kind enough to share her experience of working at a private company in their Seoul office:

A Day in the Life

I am currently working at Kiehl's, one of the many brands of L'Oreal, the largest cosmetics company in the world. Kiehl's is a New York-based brand that started in 1851 as an apothecary. Though it has enjoyed double digit growth globally, in Korea, it is still in the process of growing. Working in a more compact department allows me to experience not only marketing but also a broad spectrum of public relations, education, merchandising, sales, customer relationship management and Internet commerce. A normal day at work starts with checking the sales of our Shinsegae Mall e-commerce site and the sales of our counters in the Galleria and Shinsegae Department Store. Afterwards I talk to our counter managers about daily sales, monthly sales targets and ongoing promotions. By mid-month I am usually working on our direct mailing campaign that we send to a select target group of customers. Toward the end of the month, my duties are more focused on public relations. I compile press kits and material that will best communicate to beauty editors what is news worthy about Kiehl's. As a non-advertising brand, I usually have lunch with editors once a month to solidify our press relationships. With each month's new product launch, I have to manage the stock and forecast our stock usage for future months. This forecasting is based on analyses of current promotions I have devised to push certain products, on last year's sales and on general market trends. I will also be visiting the counters to educate our Kiehl's Customer Representatives about new products as well as to check on our merchandising, an important visual communication tool.

Chapter 11 Resources for Researching the First Professional Job

Job Search Websites and Recruiting Firms

Global:

- Monster: www.monster.com
- International Monster: http://workabroad.monster.com
- The Riley Guide: Resources for International Job Opportunities: www.rileyguide.com/internat.html
- Transitions Abroad: The Guide to Learning, Living, and Working Overseas: www.transitionsabroad.com
- Job Seeker: www.jobseeker.com
- Egon Zehnder: www.egonzehnder.com/
- Heidrick & Struggles: www.heidrick.com/default.aspx
- Hudson: www.jobs.hudson.com
- Korn/Ferry: www.kornferry.com
- Career Builder: www.careerbuilder.com

The Wall Street Journal's Career Journal:

- www.careerjournal.com

This is a treasure trove of information on job searching and career development. Regular columns include:

Diary of a Job Search **by Tim Johnston,** Careers Q&A **by Perri Capell**, In The Lead **by Carol Hymowitz,**

Work & Family **by Sue Shellenbarger,** Cubicle Culture **by Jared Sandberg,**

Managing Your Career **by Joann Lublin,** Moving On **by Jeffrey Zaslow**

CareerJournal.com has some internationally-focused articles, such as:

"A Good Career Move Means a Job in Asia" By Erin White

"A Trip Abroad Can Help You Win a Job" By Kevin Voigt

"Diversity Creates Demand For Transcultural Managers" By Pepi Sappal

"How to Create a Resume For Foreign Markets" By Myriam-Rose Kohn

Job Search Websites and Recruiting Firms

Asia, generally:

- Garner International: www.garnerasia.com/index.html
- The People at Work:www.thepeopleatwork.com/in_services.htm
- Jobstreet: www.jobstreet.com
- Jobsdb: www.jobsdb.com
- Michael Page International: www.michaelpage.com
- Job Hunter: www.j-hunter.com
- Robert Walters: www.robertwalters.com

Australia:

- Australia search engine: www.careersonline.com.au
- Australian JobSearch: http://jobsearch.gov.au
- CareerOne: www.careerone.com.au

- Craigs List: www.craigslist.org
- MyCareer.com: www.mycareer.com.au
- SEEK IT: http://it.seek.com.au

***China*:**

- Whaopin.com: www.zhaopin.com
- JobMarket: www.jobmarket-online.com
- World Work: www.worldwork.com.cn
- employchina.com: www.epchina.net
- Teach in China: www.teach-in-china.com
- Manpower China: www.manpowerprc.com.cn

***Hong Kong*:**

- South China Morning Post: www.classifiedpost.com/jshome. php
- Monster in Hong Kong: www.monster.com.hk
- HK Jobs: www.hkjobs.com
- Gemini Personnel Limited: wwwgemini.com.hk
- Manpower Hong Kong: www.manpower.com.hk

***Korea (in Korean language)*:**

- Job Korea: www.jobkorea.co.kr
- Incruit: www.incruit.co.kr
- People and Job: www.peoplenjob.com
- Saramin: www.saramin.co.kr
- Korean Government: www.work.go.kr
- Scout: www.scout.co.kr
- Career Korea: www.career.co.kr
- Humanpia: www.humanpia.co.kr

- Recruit Korea: www.recruit.co.kr
- Joblink Korea: www.joblink.co.kr
- Powerjob: www.powerjob.co.kr
- Daum Jobs: http://job.daum.net

***Japan*:**

- Yahoo! Japan: www.yahoo.co.jp
- International Career Information, Inc.: www.rici.com
- Japan Information Resource Center: www.konradh.net/jp.html
- Allied Employment Consulting (AEC) Japan: www.aecjpn.com
- Job Dragon: www.jobdragon.co.jp
- Career Cross Japan: www.careercorss.com
- Work in Japan: www.workinjapan.com
- Gaijin Pot: http://gaijinpot.com
- Recruit: http://job.rnet.or.jp
- English Resource: www.englishresource.com
- Japan Times Online: www.japantimes.co.jp

***Singapore*:**

- Achieve Career Human Resource Consultancy:
- www.achievecareer.com/
- AsiaOne Careers: http://careers.asia1.com.sg
- RecruitAsia: www.recruitasia.com
- Jobs Central: www.jobscentral.com.sg

***Europe*:**

- EuroJobs: www.eurojobs.com
- Stepstone: www.stepstone.com

- Talent4Europe: www.talent4europe.com
- Jobline: www.joblin.org
- Jobserve Sales & Marketing: www.sales.jobserve.com
- Executive Jobs: www.executive.ch
- CDS International: www.cdsintl.org
- Eurograduate: www.eurograduate.com
- Track International: www.trackint.com
- IrishJobs.ie: www.exp.ie

International Organizations

Careers in International Affairs, Seventh Edition, School of Foreign Service, Georgetown University (2004)

The United Nations:

UN e-Staffing System:
https://jobs.un.org/Galaxy/Release3/vacancy/vacancy.aspx

- UN Organization current listings:
  www.un.org/Depts/OHRM/indexpo.htm
- UN Jobs (not affiliated with UN): http://unjobs.org/
- UN Competitive Exam:
  https://jobs.un.org/elearn/production/home.html
- UN Headquarters Internship Programme:
  www.un.org/Depts/OHRM/examin/internsh/intern.htm
- G-level positions in the UN system:
  www.un.org/Depts/OHRM/salaries_allowances/salary.htm#gs

***The World Trade Organization*:** www.wto.org

***The World Bank*:** www.worldbank.org

Young Professional Program (YPP)

***The World Intellectual Property Organization*:**

www.wipo.org

***Asian Development Bank*:** www.adb.org

Young Professionals Program

***Center for Strategic and International Studies*:**

www.csis.org/about/jobs_interns/

Teaching

- Dave's ESL Cafe: www.eslcafe.com/jobs
- Japan Exchange and Teaching Program: www.mofa.go.jp/j_info/visit/jet
- Transitions Abroad: www.transitionsabroad.com/listings/work/index.shtml
- World Teach: www.worldteach.org

Study Abroad Programs

- Academic Year and Short-Term Study Abroad (New York: Institute of International Education) www.iiepassport.org
- Peterson's Study Abroad: A Guide to Semester, Summer, and Academic Year Abroad Programs www.petersons.com
- World Learning School for International Training, www.sit.edu/gp

Global Social Work and NGOs

- "International Social Work – Go Global!," www.socialworktoday.com/archive/swt_0105p14.htm
- Cross Cultural Solutions, www.crossculturalsolutions.org
- Doctors Without Borders, www.dwb.org
- George Warren Brown SSW's Social Work and Social Services Jobs Online, Washington University, http://gwbweb.wustl.edu/jobs
- Idealist, www.idealist.org
- InterAction Member Profiles, www.interaction.org
- Foundation for Sustainable Development www.fsdinternational.org
- Madre: International Human Right Organization, www.madre.org
- Relief Web, www.reliefweb.int/w/rwb.nsf (UN-project)
- Social Work Action Team (SWAT), www.swatjobs.com
- University of Texas at Austin's Service Leader, www.service leader.org
- OXFAM www.oxfamamerica.org/International Partnership for Service Learning www.ipsl.org
- Peace Corps www.peacecorps.gov
- Project HOPE www.projecthope.org
- Save the Children www.savethechildren.org
- SCI-International Voluntary Service www.sci-ivs.org
- University of Minnesota Learning Abroad Center www.uma broad.umn.edu/
- University of Michigan International Center, http://www.umich. edu/~icenter/index.html
- Visions in Action www.visionsinaction.org
- Volunteers for Peace (VFP) www.vfp.org
- YMCA, YWCA www.ymcaworldservice.org
- Volunteer and Interships – Global Crossroad, www.globalcross road.com

Salary and Compensation Information

- *The Wall Street Journal's* Career Journal pages: www.careerjournal.com

- Vault Salary Channel: www.vault.com *This is another treasure trove, including a "salary wizard" that searches by job title and geographic location so you can compare the impact of place as well as job.*

Vault Salary Surveys

– Accounting Salaries

– Consulting Salaries

– Customer Service Salaries

– Electrical Engineering Salaries

– Investment Banking Salaries

– Pharmaceutical Salaries

– Marketing Management Salaries

– Nursing Salaries

– Sales/Account Management Salaries

– Teacher Salaries

– Browse all Industries

– Browse all Functions

- **Vault Salary Central**

– Law Firm Salary Central

– Consulting Salary Central

– Finance Salary Central

- **Salary Negotiation Articles**
- **Benefits & Perks Articles**
- **Personal Finance Articles**
- **Job Search Message Boards**

First Jobs in Famous Careers

A *Forbes* feature in Spring 2006 on its insightful and fact-filled "Work" channel at www.forbes.com/work. See also *Forbes'* Work Special, "Work Around the World."

Ex-Disney CEO Michael Eisner	Futurist Alvin Toffler
Former Secretary of State Madeline Albright	Humorist Todd Hanson
Real Estate Mogul Donald Trump	Basketball Great Isiah Thomas
Legal Eagle Alan Dershowitz	Hip-Hop Entrepreneur Russell Simmons
Yankees Owner George Steinbrenner	Beach Boy Al Jardine
Rock Star Gene Simmons	Litigator David Boies
Artist Jeff Koons	Thinker Steven Pinker
Ex-Disney CEO Michael Eisner	Baseball Legend Cal Ripken, Jr.
Former Secretary of State Madeline Albright	Career Guru Richard Nelson Bolles
Real Estate Mogul Donald Trump	TV Pundit Nancy Grace

Compare Salaries and Hours Worked for Various Professions in One Market

Source: U.S. Bureau of Labor Statistics National Compensation Survey, 2004 (www.bls.gov/opub/cwc/tables)

Annual earnings of full-time workers, U.S. National Compensation Survey, July 2004

Occupation	Mean annual earnings in US $	Mean annual hours
Physicians	$128,689	2243
Airplane pilots and navigators	128,406	1083
Medical science teachers	121,230	2276
Judges	118,134	2058
Optometrists	116,403	1975
Lawyers	105,716	2174
Managers, marketing, advertising, and public relations	103,704	2131
Chief executives and general admin., public administration	102,405	2057
Economics teachers	99,516	1555
Securities and financial services sales occupations	94,005	2068
Announcers	93,112	1938
Engineering teachers	92,358	1618
Petroleum engineers	89,981	2080
Law teachers	89,947	1526
Pharmacists	88,168	2065
Aerospace engineers	85,574	2083
Dentists	82,437	2142
Managers and administrators, n.e.c.	80,871	2142
Physicists and astronomers	80,039	2072

Occupation	Mean annual earnings in US $	Mean annual hours
Electrical and electronic engineers	79,211	2117
Chemical engineers	78,645	2071
Financial managers	78,410	2105
Sales engineers	77,664	2171
Physics teachers	77,509	1442
Nuclear engineers	77,225	2080
Earth, environmental, and marine science teachers	76,353	1440
Engineers, n.e.c.	76,307	2085
Operations and systems researchers and analysts	73,460	2078
Computer systems analysts and scientists	73,327	2085
Health diagnosing practitioners, n.e.c.	72,453	2084
Other financial officers	72,319	2085
Actuaries	72,088	2179
Biological science teachers	71,935	1722
Economists	71,672	2171
Sociology teachers	71,656	1609
Physicians' assistants	71,297	2083
Managers, medicine and health	70,871	2078
Geologists and geodesists	70,665	2131
Personnel and labor relations managers	70,283	2073
Health specialties teachers	70,120	1720
Administrators, education and related fields	68,765	1912
English teachers	68,694	1540
Supervisors, firefighting and fire prevention occupations	68,673	2533
Technical writers	68,601	2103

The Best Companies to Work For

Best Companies by Lifestyle Measures and other metrics (employee satisfaction approach):

- *Fortune* magazine's 2006 "List of 100 Best Companies to Work For", based on employee interviews of U.S. employees: http://money.cnn.com/magazines/fortune/bestcompanies/
- *The Sunday Times* 100 Best Companies to Work For in the UK: http://business.timesonline.co.uk/section/0,,12190,00.html
- Great Place to Work Institute's "International Best Companies": http://www.greatplacetowork.com/best/index.php;
- *Working Mother* magazine's rating of Best Companies, measured by benefits for families and atmosphere for women employees, etc; the survey is US-based and many of the companies listed have international locations: http://www.workingmother.com/list.shtml

The Best Companies by Economic Measures (biggest (by revenues), or best-performing (profitability)):

- Forbes International 500: http://www.forbes.com/2003/07/07/internationaland.html
- Business Week Best Performers of 2006: http://msnbci.businessweek.com/magazine/toc/06_14/B397806bw50.htm

The Best Companies to Work for in Asia:

- India, www.growtalent.com
- Japan, www.greatplacetowork.jp
- Korea, www.eltechtrust.com

Investment Banking – Financial Services

- I-bank Jobs & Careers: http://www.vault.com/hubs/501/channelhome_501.jsp?ch_id=240
- Top i-banks: http://fisher.osu.edu/fin/cern/invbank.htm
- Careers in Finance: http://www.careers-in-finance.com/ib.htm
- Thomson Financial: http://www.thomson.com/financial/fi_investbank.jsp
- Private Equity firms, http://www.privateequity.com/organization
- Banking careers: http://www.careers.ed.ac.uk/STUDENTS/Careers/J7.html
- Global eFinancial Careers: http://www.efinancialcareers.co.uk/
- Banking & Finance Job Search: http://banking-finance.careerbuilder.com

Some top firms to consider:

ABN Amro Bank	Bank of America
Citigroup	Credit Suisse
Deutsche Bank	Goldman Sachs
HSBC	JPMorgan Chase
Lehman Brothers	Merrill Lynch
Morgan Stanley	RBC Capital Markets
Nomura Securities	UBS

Consulting Firms – Management, Strategy

- Vault rankings: www.vault.com/nr/consulting_rankings
- Careers in Business: www.careers-in-business.com/consulting/mc.htm
- The Harvard Business School Guide to Careers in Management Consulting 2001, Harvard Business School Publishing
- Management Consulting: A Complete Guide to the Industry. By S. Biswas and D. Twitchell.
- Institute of Management Consultants: www.imcusa.org/
- Harvard Business School Consulting Club: http://sa.hbs.edu/mconsult/
- McKinsey Quarterly: www.mckinseyquarterly.com/
- Career Guide to the Top Consulting Firms by Michael K. Norris
- Vault Career Guide to Consulting
- The Wharton M.B.A. Case Interview Study Guide: Vol. I and Vol. II, by Wharton M.B.A. Students.
- Careers in International Affairs (Seventh Edition), School of Foreign Service, Georgetown University, 2003.

Some top firms to consider:

Accenture	KPMG Consulting
Bain & Company	McKinsey & Company
Booz Allen Hamilton	Mercer Management Consulting
Boston Consulting Group	Monitor Group
Cap Gemini Ernst & Young	PwC Consulting
Deloitte Consulting	KPMG Consulting

Part III

Graduate School

Chapter 12 Should I Go to Graduate School?

"With all thy getting, get understanding."
– Proverbs

Q1: Parents and others advise us to go to graduate school if we don't know what to do (and have absolutely no idea what career to choose,) but we're close to graduating. What's more important – getting more experience at work or in graduate school?

A1: Using graduate school as a way to put off going into the marketplace is a well-known strategy, but the wisdom of doing so is not very clear. First of all, you incur a huge cost in terms of paying for tuition and other out-of-pocket expenses. You also incur a major opportunity cost: money that you could have been making somewere else but did not. At the same time, if you are just going through the motions of learning, going to graduate school does not really add much value. If you decide to go to graduate school it is much better if you know exactly why you are going. I do not like the idea of saying, "I don't know what I want to do and therefore I'm going to graduate school."

Let me offer some other alternatives: (i) go to work at any company – see what the professional setting is like; (ii) travel around the world, broaden your horizons, get more experience and meet interesting people – if you have the time and resources or can find a program that will fund the adventure (such as teaching or volunteer activities organized through charitable organizations or religious organizations); (iii) be an activist – join a cause or group that you find meaningful, so that you belong to some kind of organization. These alternatives may not directly contribute to your career development. But I think that they will allow you to learn much about communication, about working with other people and about how the world really works. Just using graduate school to delay making a decision is not something that I personally find useful.

Q2: In college, I received a broad-based social sciences education. Should I go to graduate school to focus on a more specific field? I am concerned that in my undergraduate courses, we put our feet in the water a little bit but we really didn't go swimming in the ocean…

A2: If you know of a narrow or focused field that you would like to study, then you can start your graduate school search (or job search) at a much deeper, more focused level. If you have a certain field in mind and you think that is what you want to do in your professional career, by all means, go to graduate school and get the credentials you need to enter the field. You are one of the lucky ones who knows what she wants to do. Go for it!

Q3: I want to go to graduate school, but I don't know when. Is it better to gain some experience working in the real world before I go to graduate school? Some people say it's better to go right after college because studying is fresh in your mind – they recommend we go and study while we're young and before we get distracted with work and earning money. What

do you recommend?

A3: It depends on what kind of graduate school. If your goal is to complete an M.B.A., you usually need at least three years of full-time job experience. Law school and Ph.D. programs are different – for example you can go straight to law school even though some say that it is very helpful to have job experience. See more details in the M.B.A. and Law School sections below.

Q4: If I cannot get a good job right out of college, should I go to a prestigious Master's degree program instead of taking an unattractive job?

A4: Yes. Even if the market does not highly value the content (*what* you learn) in the Master's program (for example, if it is basically a continuation of an undergraduate education instead of a professional degree program), employers will use the Master's degree to *screen* for other qualities. For example, the fact that you studied at a very good university in a challenging program may get you noticed, whereas your undergraduate institution was not in the employer's profile.

Q5: What are some of the advantages of working first if I know I want to complete a graduate level education in the near future?

A5: After your Bachelor's degree, you can look for a job with a big company that offers support for your graduate education. There are quite a few good programs that companies make available if you stay employed there for a few years. For example, they may support your graduate school tuition expense, offer time off to study, and/or have a promotion track that allows you to advance within the company after you complete the degree. There also are many companies with in-house education programs: GE has GE University, Fedex has Fedex University, etc. These "corporate universities" are a great resource for your further education, and they benefit you as well as the company. Look for these programs when you are looking at companies and applying for early-career jobs.

Q6: How do I sort through the many schools and geographic locations out there?

A6: You want to be strategic in your selection. If everybody in your home market is going to America to study, it may not be a bad idea to go to the U.K. and come back with a U.K. degree because it represents something different. If you think China is going to do very well in the future, then why not go to China and make friends there, build a great network, learn the culture, the language, and become a partial China expert when you return? It is good to be strategic and graduate school offers that opportunity geographically. There are obviously many schools in America, so that is one of the first places you would look. On the other hand, I think that there are very interesting programs all over the world. The great thing about having the Internet is that you do not have to have friends in those countries – you can just look at the programs and get a great deal of information about the programs, including how they rank in comparison to others. Do your research. If possible, try to bring back a degree that is special.

For education at the post-graduate level, there are a variety of graduate schools. Graduate schools fall generally into two categories: (i) professional schools that equip students with the skills required to enter a profession (such as business school (M.B.A.), law school (J.D.) or public policy school (M.P.A.), and (ii) academic graduate school (Ph.D.), which generally leads a person into an academic career or other jobs for which a Ph.D. is required or useful.

Q7: I enjoyed a negotiation workshop in which I participated as an undergraduate. Is there a graduate program or professional field that emphasizes these types of skills?

A7: Sure, there are many programs that train you in negotiations or conflict resolution. Several careers and professional schools can help you develop that skill set. Many graduate schools in public policy or international studies stress negotiations and conflict resolution as being important aspects of their programs in the context of diplomacy and foreign relations (see Master's degrees section below). Law schools also offer negotiations courses and mock debates. In fact, law school education and the entire legal profession are based on negotiation on behalf of clients who are in adversarial situations (see the Law School section below). You will find law firms also encourage their attorneys to maintain and improve their negotiating skills, as do members of the diplomatic corps.

It might be an unnecessarily narrow focus to study in a two-year conflict resolutions program. It is probably better to use this interest to sharpen your skill set in a public policy or law school graduate program which includes a negotiations/conflict resolution workshop or course in the curriculum. Your interest in this area indicates you would probably enjoy the public policy or legal fields.

Q8: What standardized tests are required for graduate school and when should I take them?

A8: In the U.S., Business School requires the GMAT, Law School requires the LSAT, and other graduate programs require the

GRE. Information about these exams can be found on websites for any of these graduate programs, and you must confirm the current test required by each graduate school. Outside the U.S., the testing requirements may be different, or may be in another language.

When I started thinking about going to business school, I was in my senior year. That is when I prepared for the GMAT. The junior year is probably the best time to sign up for the standardized tests and study for them because you do not yet have the pressure of senior year. It is best to get your test score in time to see which schools you qualify for (the schools publish profiles of the grades and test scores on average or in a range format for their accepted classes) and organize your applications accordingly.

Q9: When are graduate school applications due?

A9: For many nations the school year begins in the fall (early September) and ends in the spring (late May). Applications for the new class that will enter in the fall are due some time in the preceding winter – usually starting with early admissions programs in November/December and regular admissions deadlines for applications in January.

Q10: What kind of information is required to complete graduate school applications?

A10: Grades (official transcript), test score, personal statement or other essays and recommendation letters. It takes several weeks to line up this information, so start early. The personal statement or essays you write should be read by a professor or at least a couple of friends to check on grammar basics and effect. Your readers should also comment on whether they feel your essays are original, compelling and unique enough to stand out from the crowd.

Q11: In the U.S. is there a quota (limit or spaces reserved) or affirmative action program that benefits international students applying to graduate schools?

A11: You find a large contingent of international students in many top programs. Most forms of quotas are now considered illegal discrimination on the basis of race in the U.S. This may not be the case in other countries. However, each department and each university tries hard to achieve a certain amount of diversity in their accepted graduate schools classes. If they feel there are too many students in the economics department from the same country of origin, then they will probably limit additional acceptances from that country and may favor (or focus their recruiting on) citizens of other nations.

Affirmative action does not necessarily apply to foreign students – it is a policy meant to create opportunities for higher education for the benefit of groups who were disadvantaged in their earlier educational or socio-economic opportunities. Traditionally, graduate programs have tried to attract foreign students, and this has given foreign applicants a good opportunity in the admissions game; however, in the age of war on terrorism and university budget constraints, foreign applicants may face a higher degree of scrutiny or greater hurdles than nationals, at least with respect to obtaining a student visa.

Q12: In applying to graduate schools, what will be the impact of my university's grading scale? My undergraduate institution forces a curve so that my grade may be relatively high in my class, but appears low compared to other students whose

grades are inflated (i.e., their schools give out a lot of A's). Does this work to my disadvantage in admissions decisions at schools abroad?

A12: Grade inflation occurs to some extent in many places around the world and in many different universities. A curve is applied strictly in some schools and not at all in others. Schools get reputations for having grade inflation or grading according to a curve. There probably is some confusion or unfairness in the market for graduate schools when a student from a grade-inflation school is compared to a student from an institution that grades on a stricter curve.

Where the schools are well-known, the reputation will influence the meaning of the grade. Graduate admissions offices literally have a grade-adjuster that they apply to the grades of applicants, based on the undergraduate institution and its quality/reputation and grading system. However, their knowledge about grades may not extend to foreign schools – they may have no idea about the quality or rank of your undergraduate institution. In that case, you should provide some information and possibly mention that grades at your school were based on a curve.

Q13: What if my university is not well-known in a foreign country where I want to apply to graduate school?

A13: Your concern is valid: for a less-known foreign school, grades may be given less weight in the admissions decision, because they are less reliable. As an applicant, you should augment the basic grade information you supply to make your case. The quality of the institution from which the grade comes is probably very important. The rank in the class is probably very important. It will help if you can emphasize your high class rank on the application form ("GPA=3.2, top 10% of graduating class") when the grade is not that informative, or if you feel the grade is less competitive with other candidates coming from more inflated grading environments.

Q14: How important are my undergraduate grades for graduate admissions? How can my grades be compared to other applicants from other nations?

A14: Grades are important but different institutions have different policies and customs for giving grades. An East-Asian student's grades may not be comparable to those of a student from a European or a South-East Asian university. It's just too hard to compare apples and oranges. Schools earn reputations for giving easy grades or giving very tough grades, but you cannot necessarily rely on that to help you out.

The best thing to do is have a very well-written recommendation, as the recommendation letter will indicate the quality of the faculty to some degree. Also, you can ask someone who is writing the recommendation to explain how the grading system works at your school. The letter can explain that the applicant has a certain GPA, that the GPA is considered outstanding at the university (in the top x%), and that the university has a certain reputation, or something along these lines. You and your recommender need to put it all in context. Admissions folks read recommendation letters very carefully, so it's worth getting a long, careful recommendation if you have anything special to point out. Use a proactive approach to marketing yourself rather than expecting the graduate school to know what the numbers mean at an overseas institution.

Q15: Are standardized test scores important to foreign graduate

schools or employers?

A15: Yes. Standardized test scores can be helpful to even the playing field among national and foreign applicants, helping foreign students illustrate their capabilities in a scoring system the graduate school understands. Especially if the graduate school does not have good or full information about the undergraduate institution, a great test score can alleviate concerns. Employers may look back to standardized test scores when they do not have much familiarity with the quality of the degree-granting institution, but they want to consider the candidate. Standardized test scores, while not perfect indicators, are much relied upon by admissions offices and employers where the quality of the other information is less reliable.

Q16: As a foreign student walking into a classroom full of people who all seem somewhat alike I feel like I stand out in a negative way. This situation can inspire feelings of inferiority or intimidation. What are some ways to conquer this fear in an educational setting?

A16: "There is nothing to fear but fear itself." It is wise to understand the source of your fear. It is wiser to understand why it is unfounded, and to get over it – the sooner the better.

Many students find that after they have spent a week or two in the same room with this very intimidating group of people – no matter how loud or confident they may appear at first impression – there turns out to be no sound basis for any intimidation. In fact, the best of hopes is that a few of them will impress you enough that you may want to invest some of your time in a study group or out on the town with them. Remember, they came through the same admissions process you did. They have the same need to obtain the education for which you are all sitting in this room. They have ambitions and concerns similar to yours. They are merely fellow travelers, and they are most likely (certainly they should be) as concerned about what you think of them as you are about what they think of you. Certainly, never let the physical appearances of a crowd of people make a deep impression on you. What counts is below the skin, especially in graduate school. Trust yourself to handle the challenges of your educational experience, and trust that your admissions decision was not a mistake. Learn this trust now and use it again and again when you face that room full of unfamiliar people. There will always be another room full of unfamiliar people in your future professional career.

Chapter 13 Master's Degrees in Public Policy and International Affairs

Chapter 13A: *Public Administration and Public Policy Schools*

Q1: What is public policy school about? What is the focus of this type of Master's program?

A1: Public policy schools are professional graduate school designed to educate students for careers in public service. This education is broad and inter-disciplinary, including the opportunity to concentrate and focus in a particular areas of study. The topics covered include politics, history, economics, management and a wide range of specialized courses that allow the student to build a concentration in a particular area that is typically administered by a government agency, or in a particular policy area.

Q2: What is the M.P.A. degree?

A2: It is a Masters of Public Administration degree. This is a professional degree preparing university graduates for a career in public sector (government) service at a management level. A M.P.A. degree holder will be qualified to do policy work and to administer government-run programs of a wide variety, such as social welfare projects, education, fiscal planning and other government functions. Public service includes work for local, provincial/state and national levels of government; also work for inter-governmental institutions, non-profit and/or non-government organizations and others devoted to public service (as distinct from commercial or for-profit activities). M.P.A. courses usually include human resource management, budgeting and other financial/accounting functions relevant to the public sector, policy and program planning, background on political and legal institutions and issues, social issues, ethics and various areas of concentration. For more specific information on the M.P.A., see www.naspaa.org/students/faq/ faq.asp.

Q3: What is the M.P.P. degree?

A3: It is a Masters degree in Public Policy. Public policy problems, and their potential solutions, are the work of the M.P.P. program. Often combined with a law degree or M.P.A., the M.P.P. offers students background in the economic and social issues addressed by government policies and public sector organizations. Courses usually include history, economics, statistics, research and analysis methods, public finance and public sector management. M.P.P. degree holders work in think tanks and research institutions, government agencies, political action groups and other public service organizations as well as private sector companies. More information is available at www.naspaa.org/students/faq/faq.asp.

Q4: Why would I choose to pursue this type of Master's degree? Is it worth the time and tuition?

A4: They want to upgrade their academic credentials with an eye toward going into the public sector (government employment as an administrator or policy-maker), think tank or other organization that involves work on policy issues. They are not committing at this time to completing a Ph.D. These Master's degrees generally are not the first part of a Ph.D. program; rather, they are degrees that stand on their own. After one or two years' work on the Master's degree, the graduate usually has earned a credential that qualifies them for more advanced work, a more ambitious career path, and greatly improved access to top quality employers around the globe. Like the M.B.A. and other graduate degrees, the Master's in public administration or public policy comes at the opportunity cost of the tuition (high) and years of work. However, many students find the Master's degree in public policy to be a good fit with undergraduate work in politics/government, international relations, economics or business administration. The Master's years in a public policy school expose students to major current issues and opportunities to specialize in a particular field. This specialization can lead to good first jobs in research or advocacy, or in the public sector, for which the student is well-prepared after in-depth graduate level study. The best programs have excellent alumni networks, including many prominent politicians and scholars.

Q5: Is it a good idea to combine an M.P.A./M.P.P. with a law or business degree?

A5: Yes, and it is often done. The public affairs Master's degree usually will add one year to the total term of study for the two graduate degrees. However, double degree graduates report that they have more career options and deeper knowledge of their fields, and that this serves them well throughout their careers. An example is a law student who also received her M.P.A. She then took a first job in welfare policy at the state welfare agency at a time when welfare policy was being re-written. After two years in that position and implementing major policy changes, she took a different job with the state legislature writing new statutes. Both the policy experience and the law degree were prerequisites to this very responsible position drafting legislation. Starting salaries, however, do not tend to rise with the additional degree.

Q6: What types of specializations or concentrations are available? What are these policy areas?

A6: Some samples from the U.S. News & World Report's graduate schools report include City Management and Urban Policy, Environmental Policy and Management, Health Policy and Management, Information and Technology Management, Nonprofit Management, Public Finance & Budgeting, Public Management Administration, Public Policy Analysis, and Social Policy. (Source: www.usnews.com/usnews.edu.grad)

Q7: Is there a standardized test required to enter a Public Policy Master's program?

A7: Yes, the GRE. See www.usnews.com/usnews/edu/grad/articles/brief/bctests_brief.php#gre.

Q8: Are there many foreign or international students in the U.S. public policy masters programs?

A8: Yes. Check out the websites of each school (you can find a list of schools in the Resources section below). A particularly interesting one is Harvard's Kennedy School of Government, where over 50% of the students in several of the Master's programs are international students: www.ksg.harvard.edu/apply/comparison.htm. Like business, public policy and administration are global fields. In fact, study abroad opportunities are also built into many of these programs.

Chapter 13B:
International Affairs and International Studies Schools

Q1: What are international affairs and international studies Master's programs?

A1: They are professional graduate schools focused on international politics, diplomacy, business, trade, law, area studies and other international issues. Graduate programs in these fields vary considerably in their structure and course offerings. Many of them offer specializations, similar to public policy programs within the bounds of internationally applicable fields.

Q2: Are all these programs just in the U.S.?

A2: No, they are in Europe and Asia too, and growing. Check out the lists of graduate schools of international studies in the Resources at the end of this chapter.

Q3: What kinds of courses are offered at international studies schools?

A3: International studies/international affairs curriculum generally offers a broad range of courses in a several academic disciplines, including political science, economics and history, and the assortment differs among schools. Some programs have a greater focus on diplomacy/security matters, and others in economic policy; some programs have regional concentrations and area studies available, whereas others may be global in perspective and lacking in certain concentrations. Courses generally will include a broad-based core or foundation series of history, international relations, international law, policy analysis and research methods, statistics and quantitative methods and economics. The Association of Professional Schools of International Affairs (APSIA) explains that its member schools "enable students to specialize or concentrate in either functional subjects, such as international conflict resolution, international trade and finance, environmental issues, and foreign policy, or in regional areas such as Africa, Asia, the Americas, Europe, the Middle East and Russia/ Central Eurasia." APSIA schools also provide "some type of capstone experience – a comprehensive exam, thesis, internship, or independent study project – that enables students to integrate the various components of their education." (source: www.apsia.org/apsia/index.php)

Q4: What kinds of employers hire international studies graduates?

A4: International organizations (such as the United Nations, World Bank and OECD), national governments in foreign affairs agencies, NGOs (such as Amnesty International), research organizations, consulting firms, other private companies – any organization looking for new hires with a global perspective. The Association of Professional Schools of International Affairs offers the following list of employers who are interested in their graduates:

• banking and financial institutions • colleges and universities • consulting firms • cultural and educational exchange organizations • development assistance programs • federal, state and local governments	• media outlets • non-governmental organizations • policy research centers • private voluntary organizations • trade associations • transnational corporations • international organizations

(Source: www.apsia.org/apsia/index.php)

Resources for Researching Master's Degrees in Public Policy and International Affairs

Public Policy Schools

Public Policy masters degree listings:
www.gradschools.com/listings/menus/pubpol_menu.html

U.S. National Association of Schools of Public Affairs and Administration: www.naspaa.org/students/faq/faq.asp

2004 U.S. Rankings in U.S. News & World Report (www.usnews/usnews/edu/grad):

Rank	School
1.	Syracuse University (NY)
2.	Harvard University (MA)
3.	Indiana University–Bloomington

International Affairs Schools

International Studies Association: www.isanet.org/

Association of Professional Schools of International Affairs:
www.apsia.org/apsia/index.php

In the Americas:

American University	School of International Service
Carleton University	Norman Paterson School of International Affairs
Columbia University	School of International and Public Affairs
Duke University	Terry Sanford Institute of Public Policy
George Washington University	Elliott School of International Affairs
Georgetown University	Edmund A. Walsh School of Foreign Service
Harvard University	John F. Kennedy School of Government
Johns Hopkins University	Paul H. Nitze School of Advanced International Studies
Princeton University	Woodrow Wilson School of Public and International Affairs
Syracuse University	The Maxwell School
Tufts University	The Fletcher School of Law and Diplomacy
University of California, San Diego	Graduate School of International Relations and Pacific Studies (IR/PS)
University of Denver	Graduate School of International Studies
University of Maryland	School of Public Policy
University of Michigan	Gerald R. Ford School of Public Policy
University of Minnesota	Hubert H. Humphrey Institute of Public Affairs
University of Pittsburgh	Graduate School of Public And International Affairs
University of Southern California	Annenberg School for Communication
University of Washington	Henry M. Jackson School of International Studies
Yale University	Yale Center for International and Area Studies
Department of State	National Foreign Affairs Training Center
DePaul University	International Studies Program
Florida International University	Department of International Relations

Fordham University	International Political Economy and Development Program
George Mason University	International Commerce and Policy Program
Howard University	Ralph J. Bunche International Affairs Center
Monterey Institute	Graduate School of International Policy Studies
North Carolina State University	Department of Political Science and Public Administration
Rutgers, The State University of New Jersey	Center for Global Change and Governance
Seton Hall University	John C. Whitehead School of Diplomacy and International Relations
Texas A&M University	Bush School of Government & Public Service
Thunderbird	Thunderbird, The American Graduate School of International Management
Universidad Externado de Colombia	Facultad de Finanzas, Gobierno y Relaciones Internacionales
University of Chicago	Committee on International Relations
University of Miami	Master of Arts in International Administration Program
University of Oregon	International Studies Program
University of Toronto	Munk Centre for International Studies

In Asia:

Ewha Womans University	Graduate School of International Studies
Korea University	Graduate School of International Studies
Ritsumeikan University	Graduate School of International Relations
Seoul National University	Graduate School of International Studies
International University of Japan	Graduate School of International Relations
Utsunomiya University	Graduate School of International Studies

In Europe:

Graduate Institute of International Studies	Graduate Institute of International Studies (HEI)
Institut d'Etudes Politiques de Paris	Sciences Po
London School of Economics & Political Science	International Relations Department
MGIMO University	Moscow State Institute of International Relations
St. Petersburg State University	School of International Relations
Stockholm School of Economics	Stockholm School of Economics
University of St Gallen	Master of International Affairs and Governance
King's College London	Royal Institute of International Affairs
University of Wales, Aberstwyth	Department of International Affairs
University of Geneva, Switzerland	International Affairs
University of London	School of Oriental and African Studies
University of Kent at Canterbury (and Brussels)	School of International Studies

Source : www.apsia.org

Chapter 14 Business School: the M.B.A.

Q1: I'm looking to apply to graduate school and I'm open to schools in the U.S., Europe or Asia. Is there a ranking in terms of where I should apply first? Regions where I should not apply?

A1: For business school, schools in the U.S. were the traditional top priority; M.B.A. programs in the U.S. are still getting top rankings in *Business Week* and *The Wall Street Journal*. However, Business Schools increasingly are very internationally focused, both in terms of opening campuses abroad and in their student populations. Top B-schools are now populated with a global set of young professionals. This presents a nice opportunity for you to live abroad and have a valuable experience with the time commitment limited to the two years of business school.

Schools are also somewhat regionally focused. For Asia, schools in Hong Kong and Singapore are rising to the first tier of schools anywhere in the world, and these M.B.A.s are a hot commodity among employers looking to expand in China and elsewhere in Asia.

Q2: What are the differences between M.B.A. programs in the U.S., Europe and Asia? How do I choose?

A2: While American M.B.A. programs continue to be considered prestigious and are high in demand, there are now very good M.B.A. programs internationally which are becoming known and much sought-after, especially by the largest and most global companies. In fact, an Asian or European M.B.A. may give you a competitive advantage. (See the rankings for these programs in *The Wall Street Journal* and *Business Week* in the Resources at the end of this section.) Some examples: Switzerland's IMD is very high-ranked, as well as INSEAD in France and the London Business School.

See also schools in the Netherlands, Hong Kong, Singapore and Shanghai. These schools are gaining a reputation for having well-established researchers and scholars now. Consider where you want to work: if you are interested in going to a certain country, there is probably an internationally competitive M.B.A. available from a school in that country. M.B.A. programs are getting a strong start in Korea in 2007; the current expectation is for eight full-time M.B.A. programs in Korea, with a U.S.-style program of education and tuition to match.

Q3: How much is tuition at a top-tier M.B.A. program?

A3: Check the websites listed in the Resources section for current numbers. There is some variation by national location and currency, but tuition at all excellent M.B.A. schools is very expensive. The Korean price is expected to be in the range of US$15,000 or 15,000,000 Korean won per semester; the U.S. price averages above $30,000 per year in tuition alone. You also have to factor in living expenses and the opportunity cost of not working while you are in school. But at least you will get to earn some money during a summer job. You should not plan to work during the school year when you are in a full-time M.B.A. program, as the M.B.A. program is designed to be rigorous and intensive. The social network you form from being fully involved in the M.B.A. is a very important aspect of the program.

Q4: What is an executive M.B.A.?

A4: This is a part-time M.B.A. program that allows you to complete an M.B.A. while you continue working in a full-time job. You must check out the change in job prospects based on the executive versus full-time M.B.A. program.

Q5: If I want to get an M.B.A., when do I start preparing and what should I do?

A5: First, to get into a good M.B.A. program, you have to have a good GPA, good GMAT score (the standardized test for MBA programs), recommendation letters and essays. That is the application part. But before any of that you have to have full-time job experience of at least three years.

If you are an undergraduate student now and you want to get into a very good M.B.A. program, you need patience and work experience. Your three to five years of full-time job experience should preferably be in a large multinational company or professional services firm. The work in the M.B.A. program is based on real-world experience, case studies, and group work. In a group, you have to have some kind of contribution to make based on your experience. This is where the important learning occurs, not just in the classroom. The first thing you want to do, if your mid-term goal is to get into a top M.B.A. program, is to look for a first job in a respected firm. I think that is the place to start. Of course, you have to manage your GPA well, and essays and references are all part of the package.

Q6: Are top-tier M.B.A. programs admitting only people who have worked in investment banking or consulting? What if I want to teach or pursue non-business interests in my early career – does this eliminate me from the M.B.A. ranks later on?

A6: No. M.B.A. programs want diversity in their student bodies as well as relevant business experience. They are known to admit engineers, teachers, military officers, scientists and others with high-achieving backgrounds. The firms that recruit out of the M.B.A. programs are looking for this diverse, ambitious and interesting dispersion of future employees as well, though the cultural meaning of "achievement" and "interesting" may differ geographically. The desirability of hiring from the alma maters of the firm's current employees differs as well. For example, it is common to see alumni of the same universities working at the same firms in most places around the world. In some markets, this is very concentrated. But in general, for business school admissions, the schools do not want an entering class of people from the same background. Artists, entrepreneurs and those with experience working for a local company can be in the running, as well as those with experience at big companies, banks and consulting firms.

Q7: How do I know whether going after an M.B.A. will be worth it?

A7: When you are considering whether to get an M.B.A. or any other graduate degree, you are looking at spending a significant amount of resources in time, money, and opportunity cost. Therefore it is important to look at the profile of the graduates of the graduate school. Find out what they have done with that degree. For M.B.A. programs, law schools and other graduate schools, there are rankings of the quality of the programs. The alumni network is also a critical component of the value of the degree. It is important to research not only the program of the school, but the track records of its graduates in terms of how the degree changed their careers.

In general, if you are accepted to a top tier program, you should go. Run a cost-benefit analysis over the course of your career and confirm that the returns from the investment in a top-tier graduate program outweigh the costs.

When you drop down to the next tier of schools, or you analyze the returns to an international student from studying at a less known or very local school, the cost-benefit analysis may turn out differently. Tuition may be just as high but the rewards over your career may be lower. The cost of the degree may be only slightly outweighed by the benefits and it may depend on how long you amortize that degree over your career. Your analysis is affected by how old you are when you enter the program, how long you plan to be working and the increase in salary or change in professional roles for which the degree will qualify you.

Q8: Are all business schools offering basically the same program?

A8: Various M.B.A. programs are best known for certain fields: for example, Stanford for entrepreneurship and venture capital, University of Chicago for finance, Kellogg (Northwestern) for marketing.

In addition to the regular two-year M.B.A. program, nowadays business schools have some specific programs that are tailored to specific market needs, such as one-year programs in finance. Carnegie Mellon, for example, has a one-year (highly technical) finance program as well as an information technology/management information systems program. The specialized programs do not offer the same degree as the M.B.A., but they offer a Master's degree in marketing, finance, IT, etc. If you know what you want to do, and if you are interested in a specific field, look for that kind of tailored program. It may not be a two-year full-blown M.B.A. program, but still I think it is worth it and companies are looking for people with those degrees.

Q9: Are there good scholarships for M.B.A. programs?

A9: Very few. For professional schools (business and law school), scholarships are limited. Ask each school, but do not expect the school to pay for itself. Maybe one or two students per class per year are awarded large scholarships, but generally you have to pay to get this education in professional schools.

The school's financial aid office however will be able to put together a loan package for you. This is where your cost-benefit analysis comes in: the higher salary you achieve after obtaining a professional degree usually enables you to use loans to pay for the degree. Be aware that you will be committing yourself to taking one of the higher-paying jobs upon graduation if you use debt to cover your M.B.A. expenses. For a top-tier school and also at some lesser institutions, the benefits over a career far outweigh the costs.

Resources for Researching Business Schools

Business Week on Business Schools: www.businessweek.com/bschools/index.html

"*BusinessWeek's* 2005 profiles of full-time M.B.A. programs introduce you to more than 320 M.B.A. programs around the globe"

- International Rankings: http://www.businessweek.com/bschools/04/index.html
- M.B.A. Insider (admissions): http://www.businessweek.com/bschools/M.B.A.insider/
- Profiles of 320 M.B.A. Programs world-wide: www.businessweek.com/bschools/05/geographic.htm
- China's B-School Boom: http://www.businessweek.com/bschools/china/

Asiaweek's Top Business Schools in Asia

Best Full-Time Programs (Overall)

Asiaweek's MBA Ranking: Best Full-Time Programs	
Rank	**School**
1	Melbourne Business School
2	Indian Institute of Management, Ahmedabad
3	Asian Institute of Management (Philippines)
4	Asian Institute of Technology, Thailand (School of Management)
5	NUS Business School (National University of Singapore)
6	Chinese University of Hong Kong
7	Korea Advanced Institute of Science and Technology (Graduate School of Management)
8	Macquarie Graduate School of Management (Australia)
9	Nanyang Business School (Nanyang Technological University, Singapore)
10	Sasin Graduate Institute of Business & Administration (Chulalongkorn University, Thailand)
11	Monash Mount Eliza Business School (Australia)
12	Indian Institute of Management, Bangalore
13	International University of Japan (Graduate School of Management)
14	China Europe International Business School (China)
15	National Cheng-chi University, Taiwan (College of Commerce)
16	Waseda University Graduate School of Asia Pacific Studies (Japan)
17	Brisbane Graduate School of Business (Queensland University of Technology, Australia)
18	Lahore University of Management Sciences (Pakistan)
19	University of Queensland, Australia (Graduate School of Management)
20	Seoul National University (College of Business Administration)
21	Indian Institute of Technology, Bombay (School of Management)
22	University of Adelaide, Australia (Graduate School of Management)
23	National Taiwan University of Science & Technology (College of Management)
24	University of the Philippines (College of Business Administration)
25	Curtin University of Technology, Australia (Graduate School of Business)

Source: www.pathfinder.com/asiaweek/features/mba/index.html

The Wall Street Journal on American and European Business Schools: www.collegejournal.com/mbacenter/

International Ranking : This ranking includes European, North American and Central American schools that have a global pool of recruiters. It is based on how recruiters rated each school on 20 different attributes, their future plans to recruit students from the school, and the number of countries from which it draws recruiters. To be eligible for this ranking, a school needed respondents from at least four countries.

2005 Rank	University (Business School)
1	IMD
2	ESADE Business School
3	Carnegie Mellon University
4	Instituto Panamericano de Alta Direccion de Empresa
5	University of London (London Business School)
6	University of Western Ontario (Ivey)
7	Thunderbird
8	Massachusetts Institute of Technology (Sloan)
9	INSEAD
10	INCAE
11	HEC School of Management, Paris
12	Instituto de Empresa
13	Columbia University
14	Erasmus University (Rotterdam)
15	York University (Schulich)
16	University of Chicago
17	Harvard University
18	Stanford University
19	University of Navarra (IESE)
20	Bocconi University

Source: *"The Wall Street Journal Guide to The Top Business Schools 2006" (2005, Random House Reference).*

Chapter 15 Law School: the J.D. and the LL.M.

Q1: ***My grades are just OK (top half of my class), but not stellar. I think I would like law school and a legal career. Can I get accepted at a law school in the U.S.? Which schools should I apply to? How many?***

A1: Grades matter for law school admissions. Top half of the class will be good enough to get you into a law school, but it is unlikely you would be accepted at one of the top five or ten schools without stellar grades. Thousands of undergraduates apply for law school, and there are thousands of spaces in U.S. law schools. However, acceptance rates at the 25 or so "top tier" schools are quite low. If you are in the top 5% of your class, you should apply to the top tier of schools. If your grades are lower but still respectable, apply to some of the 20 or 30 schools in the "second tier" or schools further down the rankings, depending on where your grades match the schools' profiles.

Schools publish a lot of information about their admissions process, criteria and the profiles of their accepted students (see Resources section below for where to find this important data). Your eligibility is a function of your LSAT and GPA in a composite number. If you meet the threshold numbers, then the admissions office will open your packet of application materials (reference letters, personal statement, resume) and learn more about you. If your grades and LSAT score are out of range, your nice application goes right to the "reject" pile. Apply where you have good chances of getting your application read. International students with multiple language skills, interesting life experiences and unique characteristics will be attractive candidates if they are within the acceptable range of grades/LSAT.

Q2: If I get into a "second tier" school and not an "ivy league" law school, should I attend? Am I better off without the law school degree in that case?

A2: Yes, you should attend. A law school education is a powerful thing. It changes your job prospects, your abilities and your knowledge of the world around you. With a law degree from any accredited institution, you now are eligible to work as a lawyer (after you take the local bar exam, of course) in one of many legal careers (law firm, in-house at a company, domestically or overseas where foreign-licensed lawyers can practice, in a policy-making role, teaching, etc.) Your earning power has increased. Your knowledge and understanding of risk, business, political issues, justice systems and many other important topics has developed considerably. You are part of an international profession with many opportunities. At the same time, your law degree does indicate the quality of your legal education, so it is generally advisable to go to the highest-ranking school that accepts you.

In the U.S. and internationally, you will find that your U.S. law degree is respected even if it is not from one of the top tier schools. Basically, your grades in law school matter more if you are at a lower-tier school. You should take the LSAT early so you know your score, then you combine the LSAT and GPA and you know which schools you are eligible for. You should apply to several schools, a couple of which are bit of a stretch for your grade profile, a couple of which are just within reach based on your numbers, and couple of which are "safety" schools. For the schools where you are within the usual grade/LSAT profile of admitted students, your resume and personal statement are likely to be very compelling − international background, multiple languages, high-ranked undergrad institution, etc. So go for it.

Q3: If I want to go to law school, should I work for a year or two, or is it better to go right away?

A3: Students who work for a year or two before going to law school sometimes enjoy law school more, perform better in law school, and have better success in getting their first law job. The year or two of work experience before going to law school is often sought after by law firms and other law employers because there are many students in law school who have very similar resumes and no work experience – good college, good grades in law school, but that is it (other than various extracurricular activities). When choosing between two candidates, if one of them also has one or two years (or more) of work experience, the employer is likely to choose the student with the job experience. If the job experience is high-quality, the law student may additionally have relevant skills and a better informed perspective that contributes to better work at the legal employer. All else being equal, I recommend to work a year or two before attending law school.

Q4: Why would an employer favor a law student with work experience over another law student with equally good grades?

A4: The employer is looking for a good employee, not just a good student, and is interested in how the new recruit will perform immediately, as well as over the longer term. The law firm or company may hire the student with work experience because she will probably be a little more mature. The fact that she has left a paying job to come to law school shows some dedication to the profession – that law school was not merely a default choice ("I had nothing else to do···").

The law student with work experience is likely to be more discreet or professional in their approach to colleagues and clients. She will most certainly have more realistic expectations about what it means to work a long day at a desk. Some students who have been in school all their lives may expect to be entertained at work and given exciting assignments from the first day. While that will all come with a good firm, immediately the new recruit needs to get focused on how she can add to her employer's profitability. Students with a professional work background are generally less risky than their inexperienced peers.

Q5: I am planning to go to law school. What type of undergraduate education best prepares me? Should I study law in college too?

A5: The best undergraduate background for law school is a major that teaches you to solve problems and to think critically. Philosophy is great for its focus on logic. Economics majors usually are very well equipped for law school and all kinds of corporate law practice (both litigation and transactional). History and politics are excellent, as are math and science. Engineering plus law is a great combination for patent attorneys and work with high-tech clients (and is very much in demand). Knowledge of the current law in a particular place is almost irrelevant.

If you go to law school and become a licensed attorney, you will study the law of the place where you become licensed. It would be a pity to study nothing but law all these many years of university education and not have foundational learning in basic economics, history, philosophy, math, science and languages. All these undergraduate courses contribute to your ability to think analytically about the socio-economic world to which the law applies. It is best to go to law school equipped with tools from the social sciences and hard sciences, and save law for law school.

Q6: How much legal knowledge do the law schools assume we have?

A6: A U.S. law school will assume that you have no prior knowledge of law. In fact, significant prior knowledge of law may be confusing when you are sitting in a law school classroom being taught to analyze cases and develop your legal mind. You may find it easiest simply to follow the professor's line of thinking, and not confuse your new learning experience with pre-conceived notions of how it was done or taught elsewhere.

Q7: How does the ranking of the law school affect the employment opportunities of graduates of the school? Does the law school's ranking really affect the lawyer's long-term career prospects?

A7: Yes, ranking matters. No, you will not be jobless if you go to a mid-ranked or regional/local law school. You will have a different range of employment options upon graduation. But your law school (or other graduate school) ranking will impact your resume throughout your career. It becomes less important as you accumulate other experience and signals of quality over the course of your career. Hiring is more a regional phenomenon for lower-ranking schools. For the top 15-25 law schools in the U.S., their graduates are hired at major cities across the country. For examples, law firms from Wall Street, Washington D.C., Chicago and Los Angeles regularly recruit from all the top tier law schools regardless of the school's location. However, graduates of regional schools will have plenty of job options. They may have less success getting a job from a top ranking firm in a faraway city, but a much better chance of getting a job where the school's alumni naturally flow to that region.

Q8: Do law school grades matter for getting a job as a law clerk or law associate after graduation?

A8: Yes, grades matter. Law firms and other employers such as corporations or government agencies have a profile for the candidates that they hire. Elite law firms have a list of schools (it is a relatively long list, pretty much the top tier and a few regional/local schools) from which they regularly recruit. To meet the profile (i.e., to get your resume chosen and be called in for an interview), a lower GPA at any of the top schools may get you in the door, whereas a higher GPA is required to get the interview if you come from a lower-ranked school. The final grade upon your graduation will be checked by the law firm and will impact your hiring prospects for later career moves. For the first law job, it is the usual path to get a summer clerkship (full-time employment) following the second year of law school. If all goes well you get an offer to join the firm full-time following the third year and graduation. That offer for the summer clerkship comes during recruiting season (on-campus interviews and fly-backs to meet more people at the firm for a second round) in the fall of the 2nd year. This means that the only grades the firms have to look at is your first year grades, so they matter a lot!

Q9: How are grades determined in law school? Is there a curve?

A9: For the first year of law school classes (i.e., the year when grades matter most for clerkship and law firm offers), a strict curve is applied to grades. Some say that your success (in terms of grades) is based on your fellow students' failure ··· but that is of course a terrible way to think about a learning process. You can help yourself by forming excellent study habits, figuring out how to read quickly and dissect cases, making good outlines and testing well in essay format. Many people choose to type their exams. Some law students panic when they receive the first "B" of their lives, but they quickly learn that on a normal distribution curve, a "B" is average and puts them in the middle of their class – not the death knell for a legal career, but a fair indicator of how they scored relative to the rest of their class.

Q10: What is a national law school versus a regional or state school?

A10: There are two basic styles of law school education – national and state/regional. National law schools tend to be the top-ranked schools nationally, though they may not be the preferred source of new lawyers in a given firm or town. Yale, Harvard, Stanford, University of Chicago, Georgetown, University of

Virginia, Berkeley – these are "national" schools that educate with the goal of creating the legal mind that can learn the black-letter law of any jurisdiction (which is what the newly-minted J.D. students need to become licensed in a specific jurisdiction after taking the bar exam). In the U.S., the bar exam is given, and law licensure is awarded, at the state level, not the national level. The bar exam tests for substantive knowledge of the current local law of the state, to qualify the lawyer for practice in that state.

National law schools do not teach for the bar exam. They teach general legal concepts, some legal history and legal theory that could be applicable in any U.S. jurisdiction. Regional law schools or state law schools tend to teach the law of that state, the law of that area. Many of the graduates of those law schools score higher on the bar exam because they have spent the three years of law school learning that substantive law. They are well-prepared to practice law in that jurisdiction because that is what they have been trained for. It is a different style of training with a different geographical focus and therefore a different implication for career paths in law.

Q11: Do I need to know what legal field I want to practice in before I go to law school?

A11: You do not need to know which area of law you want to practice before going to law school. You will most likely develop a feeling for that while you are in law school. I recommend taking a wide variety of courses during law school. You will find over the course of your law career that you will be naturally narrowing your field of practice. There is no need to narrow the field from the beginning. In the first year of law school (called the "1L" year) there are 5-6 required courses that form the broad foundation for legal education: criminal law, contracts, torts, property, civil procedure, constitutional law, and legal writing and research. As you can see it is very broad. In the second and third years of law school, you can take electives. During the summers, you should work for a potential post-graduation employer in a clerkship or summer associate position, most of which are offered by law firms (which pay the same monthly salary as first year lawyers, or close to it).

The 2L and 3L years and the summers offer you some exposure to different fields. Usually the firms will have you choose a couple of their practice groups to visit as a summer clerk, then you are expected to choose one practice field within the firm to join as a new hire post-graduation. While some law firms say they give a general offer from the firm, not from a particular department, the reality is that you have to choose what area of law you will learn and practice, so it is efficient to focus and make an informed decision about your general direction from the clerkship days.

After practicing for a few years, it is possible to move to related fields, but you should build a skill set within a practice area that makes you an expert. Moving practice areas means starting over to a significant degree: only some skills (writing, dealing with clients) are transferable, others are not (knowledge of the statutes and regulations for insurance or the tax code and recent tax court rulings). The first major important decision on how to focus your legal career is generally in choosing whether you will go into criminal, litigation or transactional practice.

Q12: What do young lawyers do at large firms? What is the actual work in the early years?

A12: There is a lot of editing to do and a lot of documents to review. On the litigation side, young lawyers are doing "discovery": that means they are trying to discover a needle in a haystack (some tiny bit of information in a room full of boxes). They may be reading and summarizing contracts for weeks. If the job does not seem too exciting, it is important to understand what the larger goal is. You need to understand what the litigation is all about.

Q13: Do first year lawyers end up in client meetings?

A13: Rarely. If you are not invited to sit in on a client meeting in your first year, realize that it is probably a good thing. If you joined the client meeting and you screwed up the client relationship right off the bat, you may have a very short tenure with that firm. Be patient and realize that low exposure is a safety precaution. It allows you time to figure out what is going on before you speak out in a way that is detrimental to your career and your firm. Less pressure to perform for clients or in negotiations allows you to focus on the work of developing lawyering skills. You will get there very soon and remember fondly your days of low client exposure.

Q14: I'm planning to go to either to law school or business school after I work for a few years. What kind of job should I look for now?

A14: To prepare for law school, I recommend a job outside of law practice. Develop some skills that are outside of law if you plan to spend the rest of your career practicing law. Consulting or finance experience may be helpful when a company starts looking to hire you for a specific division of a law firm, or later as in-house counsel. The company, if it is not a law firm, will operate in some industry and need for you to understand their financial priorities and risks. If you demonstrate an interest in the field of finance, then you will have an advantage in law school and in law job recruiting over other law school graduates who really have no clue, especially if they went straight from undergrad to law school. Work in any field you feel passionately about. And maybe a few months before, maybe the summer before law school, you can work as a paralegal if you are really dying to get inside a law department or law firm. In terms of doing all your work experience at a law firm, before law school, I think it is a little bit redundant.

Q15: For applying to U.S. law schools, is there an affirmative action policy or quota that helps or hurts my chances of being admitted? I am a non-U.S. citizen and an ethnic minority in the U.S.

A15: Most U.S. law school admissions processes seek to create a diverse student body. The law schools actively recruit students who will bring an ethnic and gender mix into the schools. Upon graduation from law school, most large employers (law firms, corporations, government agencies) will do the same. They seek to have a mix in their newly hired class in their male/female ratio – something usually close to fifty-fifty – and a healthy mix among ethnicities.

This is not a legal requirement. In fact, U.S. law currently considers discrimination on the basis of race or gender to be illegal discrimination. The admissions and hiring choices are to be made on the basis of merit. The result is that large schools and large firms go to significant efforts to recruit and retain women and ethnic minority candidates. This is because achieving a balanced gender and ethnic mix looks good for the school or firm. It creates the obvious evidence that the school or firm did not discriminate against women or ethnic minorities.

There are civil society groups and professional groups (like bar associations in U.S. states) that monitor how successful the law schools and the law firms and companies are at their female and minority recruitment. Where firms have not achieved a significant number of female and ethnic minority employees, they have sometimes had lawsuits based on hostile workplace allegations or negative publicity. Once hired, an employee in the U.S. has a legal right to be given equal professional opportunities based on their merit and not to be discriminated against due to their gender or ethnicity. These cultural values are represented in the graduate school admissions process as well. Because law schools, law firms and many businesses find it in their best interest to have an international appearance and to have a healthy mix of males and females throughout their ranks, sometimes international students and especially women students find themselves to have a slight advantage or more opportunity in a competitive environment due to their ability to help these institutions achieve the gender and ethnic mix they would like to achieve.

Q16: Are there good scholarships for law school?

A16: Financial aid is available primarily in the form of loans for the professional schools. To decide whether you can afford a professional graduate education mostly depends on how long you are going to work and how much more you can make in salary with the professional degree. Usually, it is a good investment. The relevant calculation is a forward-looking one (future cash flows increased by the graduate degree) and not just cash on hand. Your graduate education is an investment. Many students go to business school or law school largely by taking out personal debt (from a bank or government-sponsored student loan program). The financial aid office at each business school and law school is capable of explaining exactly what an accepted or prospective student's financial aid options are. There may be a loan package that covers the entire cost of the education. You can find that out through the financial aid office of the particular school.

Q17: Is it safe to take out student loans? What if I cannot repay them?

A17: If you decide to take out loans to get the education, then you must realize that you are committing to working at a relatively high salary, meaning working at a good firm for several years – this is called the "golden handcuffs". Additionally, there are loan deferment or forgiveness programs for law graduates who go to work in the public interest (at a far lower salary than in the private market). Some scholarships will even pay for part of law school if you commit to working in the public interest.

For some students, the loan burden is a good and effective incentive to get a good job and stay in it for long enough to pay off the debt – which is also long enough to establish your professional career with excellent training that pays dividends over the entire span of the career, in addition to paying off the student loans. Personal finance issues can help the student stay focused on performing well in school and in the early years of working. Of course, reasonable minds can differ on whether a student should take out debt to go to graduate school. To the extent that necessity is a powerful motivator, student loans can exert a powerful influence indeed.

Q18: What is an LL.M.? Does it qualify me to practice law in the U.S. or another nation?

A18: The LL.M. is the Master of Laws degree. It is an academic or specialist degree. It does not qualify you to sit for the bar exam or qualify you to practice law in any jurisdiction. It does enhance your education and it is a one-year program offered by many U.S. law schools. The LL.M. programs generally are available to students have completed their J.D. degree from a law school in the U.S. and will study in a specialized field for the LL.M., and to foreign students who studied law in university, completing the requirements to practice law in their home country. You must check on the specific requirements of the LL.M. program to assess the admissions requirements – for example, whether foreign students must be licensed to practice law in their home countries, or the precise type of degree that is required for admission.

Some law schools offer specialized graduate degree programs with a large number of graduate courses in a particular field such as taxation or securities regulation. Many LL.M. courses allow students to take any law school courses and offer the flexibility to create their own programs. Some programs allow students to compile their own selection of courses from the general law school curriculum to complete a self-designed concentration, such as "law and economics" or "comparative law." For more on LL.M. programs worldwide, check out http://www.llm-guide.com/llm-faq.

Resources for Researching Law Schools

- US News: http://www.usnews.com/usnews/edu/grad/ rankings/ law/lawindex_brief.php
- ILRG: http://www.ilrg.com/rankings.html
- LSAC (Law School Admissions Council): http://www.lsac. org/LSAC.asp?url=lsac/deans-speak-out-rankings.asp
- Princeton Review: http://www.princetonreview.com/law/ research/rankings/rankings.asp
- LLM Guide: http://www.llm-guide.com/what-is-an-llm
- AALS (Association of American Law Schools): http://www.aals.org/
- Canadian Law Schools: http://jurist.law.utoronto.ca/lawschl. htm
- UK Law Schools: http://www.law.warwick.ac.uk/lcc/ lawschools.html
- Australian & NZ Law Schools: http://www.gradschools.com/listings/ Australia/law_australia.html
- Asia Pacific Law Schools: http://www.hg.org/asiapacific-schools. html
- Law Study and Law Students: http://www.hg.org/schools. html
- Asialaw: www.asialaw.com
- Findlaw: www.findlaw.com (includes "Greedy Associates" and "Infirmation" channels re: law firms)
- Rankings: www.leiterrankings.com

Chapter 16 Academic Graduate School: the Ph.D.

Q1: I want to go to graduate school and complete a Ph.D., but I don't know when. Is it better to gain some experience working in the real world before I go to graduate school?

A1: If you are thinking about going to graduate school to complete a Ph.D., then I think for many fields the time you spend working does not contribute significantly to the Ph.D. goal. If you want to earn your Ph.D., it might be good to start right away. It takes quite a long time to finish a Ph.D.

Q2: I think I want to get a Ph.D., but it seems like it is a really big commitment. How do I know if it is worthwhile?

A2: You are right: getting a Ph.D., unfortunately, takes a long time – typically, four or five years in an American institution if you are on time. I have seen people take over twelve or fifteen years. The fastest graduates would finish in two and half year or three years, and those are extraordinary cases where the student is either exceptionally good or the school is exceptionally loose. So, you should figure on spending next four to six or more years of your life working very hard. That is a big commitment. On the other hand, certain jobs require a Ph.D. so you may not have much choice if you are dying to get one of those jobs. For example, in many institutions of higher learning, to be a faculty member you need to have a Ph.D.

Q3: I heard that some Ph.D. programs are very challenging. How do I know if I will survive?

A3: Ph.D. programs are very demanding. Clearly, some are more demanding than others. It is important to research Ph.D. programs and their level of difficulty. One good measure will be to see the drop-out rate for a particular program. Drop-outs are people who decide to leave the program for various reasons. You may be surprised to know that some graduate programs secretly delight in their high dropout rate.

A Ph.D. program requires you to pass muster in two areas: one is coursework, the other is writing a thesis. The first year of coursework is usually extremely difficult and will require great perseverance on the part of all students. Many students drop out after the first year. To mark the end of the coursework section of the program, there are usually preliminary or qualifying exams: this is another stressful phase. After passing the qualifying exams, comes the thesis writing. Some find writing their thesis highly enjoyable, whereas other students struggle. Those who enjoy it love the challenge and the creativity involved. The students who struggle are those who have a hard time coming up with a decent topic for writing such a lengthy essay. Students successful in completing the Ph.D. tend to exhibit great passion for the subject.

Q4: What happens if I drop out in the middle of the program? Will my effort be for naught?

A4: Many programs award a Master's degree to students who complete the basic coursework. There will be certain requirements for the number of credits, so it is a good idea to check your status before deciding to leave – you may be able to walk away with a Master's degree.

Q5: I heard mention of an ABD? What is that?

A5: ABD stands for "all but dissertation." It is not a formal qualification. The term is used casually to refer to students who have completed their coursework but not completed their Ph.D. thesis.

Q6: I've seen rankings of Ph.D. programs. Should the rank be important in my decision to go to a program?

A6: Ph.D. program rankings are important, especially during recruitment upon completion of your Ph.D. Employers will view certain Ph.D.'s with greater esteem than others, and may recruit only from certain top-ranking schools. Having said this, the rankings are not totally accurate. Some small departments may excel in a particular specialized field. If you know before starting a program that you are interested in a specific field, then look at the rankings for that area rather than the ranking of the whole department or university.

Q7: How do I know if I have the right personal attributes to be an academic?

A7: The stereotype associated with an academic professional is the exact opposite of Indiana Jones: boring, absent-minded, pedantic, stay-at-home, studious type. However, academia allows a great range of personality types to find their niche. Tasks in the work of an academic cross a wide spectrum from studying the past to the future; developing new ideas, criticism, writing, speaking, practical research, theoretical research, guiding students, partying with students, hiding from students, etc. Be aware that there may be no typical day in the life, as a professor's many and various roles result in work that varies. The academic calendar obviously structures the academic's work, creating flexibility around summers and winter school holidays that is rarely found in companies or agencies.

Q8: What is the job market like for Ph.D.s?

A8: The great thing about the job market for Ph.D.s is that it can be global. This means you can get a Ph.D. from a university in Australia and land a job in Britain, Nigeria or the U.S., perhaps more easily than in other professional areas. On the flip side, the local market for Ph.D.'s may be very limited. A person receiving her Ph.D. in Economics from the University of British Columbia in Vancouver may have a hard time finding a job in Vancouver and has to plan on relocating. It bears warning that this can impact your family commitments and relationships. Many universities actually refuse to hire their own Ph.D.s, so you can plan to move for your first job after receiving your Ph.D.

Q9: What can I do with a Ph.D. other than teaching?

A9: There are a lot of things that you can do with the Ph.D. that are not academically related. In some cases, a Ph.D. is a signal that you are knowledgeable about a certain area. Some think tanks, research institutions and newspaper organizations want to have some Ph.D.s on their staffs. On the other hand, many employers view a Ph.D. as being over qualified. You would be older by the time you finish your Ph.D., so you would expect to earn a higher entry-level salary, which may not be attractive to potential employers. I would be very careful about doing a Ph.D.: this should be a choice that you make because the area you study will open more doors for you. You should be aware that having a Ph.D. shuts some doors for you.

Q10: Because it costs a lot of money to study abroad, are there ways to finance overseas education, other than relying on my parents?

A10: Studying abroad is very expensive and you need to think carefully about the financing requirements. The great thing with Ph.D. programs is that there are opportunities to work as a research assistant or teaching assistant. Indeed, many students are self-supporting through their graduate school duration. There are also numerous scholarships that you can earn at the national level or from corporate donors or other groups interested in awarding scholarships. Those are the sources that you should look into.

Alternatively, you can work and study at the same time. I do not recommend that as a first option because some of these graduate programs are very demanding. To be distracted from your studies in order to work at other jobs can be very difficult for you. But many students have done that in the past and it is not something that you should rule out entirely.

Q11: Do U.S. graduate schools offer scholarships for foreign students?

A11: Many schools have substantial scholarships which they give to outstanding students. They are competitive, and some may be reserved for national citizens. Requirements vary by school and scholarship, and the specific requirements for scholarship recipients may be determined by the donor of the money.

On the other hand, many universities at the graduate school level hire teaching assistants and research assistants. The salary for this work is the basic form of financial support for graduate students. Most programs offer this work, and in many cases they do not discriminate against foreign students. If you can demonstrate the ability to be a good research assistant, and if you have good English skills so that you can conduct classes in English, then the demand for your services as a graduate student will be high. This is how most people support their financial needs during graduate study.

Q12: Are the graduate student teaching opportunities available in Europe and Asia, too?

A12: These opportunities may be more common in the U.S., especially among large state-run universities, and maybe more difficult to get in Europe. However, I think some of the European universities have very generous government support for all types of students, so you should research each country separately. On the other hand, there are some countries such as Britain which charge a lot more tuition to foreign students than to U.K. students.

Q13: How does the educational value compare, given differences in cost, among U.S., U.K., Continental European and Asian graduate schools?

A13: Having gone to graduate school in England, I think it is quite good value for the money. First, earning a masters degree took half the time for my program, which was a one-year program at the London School of Economics. On paper, it will be noted as a one-year instead of a two-year Master's degree. However, it may be only a nine-month program that lets you take three months off in the summer. Compare that to a two-year Master's program which is typical in the U.S. Also, tuition varies, based on whether you are an EU-member or a non-EU-member applicant. If you are an EU-member applicant, I think it will cost about £8,000 (approx. US$12,000) per year, for one year. Non-EU members pay more. At the end of the degree, you will have spent half the time, and half the money, to earn the same degree.

Q14: I think I'm interested in graduate school; certainly, I'd like to pursue further study and research in the field of my major from college. How do I know which graduate programs I should apply to, and which are the best in my particular field?

A14: Each academic field has its elite institutions, and some departments may be known for a particular point of view or certain areas of expertise. Your professors from college are your best resource: talk to them directly about the field. For general research, you can start with some websites that may give you an overview and rankings, then spend time looking at the particular schools. See, for starters, Thomson/Peterson's Planner: www.petersons. com/graduate_home.asp;Gradschools.com: www.grad schools.com/ ; and U.S. News & World Report, America's Best Graduate Schools 2007: http://www. usnews.com/usnews/edu/grad/rankings/rankindex_brief.php.

Chapter 17 The Application Process

Q1: Whom should I ask to write my letters of recommendation?

A1: Strong letters of recommendation can be written by someone you have worked with closely. A direct supervisor or employer can say specific good things about your personal qualities and the quality of your work. For example, if you do research for your professor, try to create some work product, be diligent, use your critical thinking skills and impress the professor. Perhaps you would like to choose a professor in whose class you received top grades. Choose a professor who you like and for whom you have performed well.

Some candidates try to get a prestigious person to write a letter of recommendation. This is a strategy that can also backfire. Although the prestigious person's signature may carry a lot of weight in a place where they are famous and well respected, if they barely know you (worst case, if they just met you through a paper introduction) then all they can possibly write is that they just met you. If they know your family, or they are willing to take time to get to know you just to write the letter, the strategy may be more successful.

Generally for graduate school applications, it is much more important that the letter of recommendation reflect your personal integrity, work skills, and habits based on as much direct work experience as possible with the person writing the letter of recommendation. An immediate supervisor from a summer job or internship (or even volunteer work) is a good person for you to ask to write your letters of recommendation because this type of supervisor can explain exactly what you did and how well you did it. They are in a position to judge your work. Peers' recommendations are less influential than those of the person to whom you reported.

Q2: For letters of recommendation, are there people with connections to my prospective university or employer who I should ask to recommend me?

A2: For letters of recommendation, in my view, there is an implicit hierarchy of the letters in terms of their value, based on who is writing them for you. For graduate school, I think the top tier recommendation letter is written by a person on the faculty of the graduate school to which you are applying. If you are applying to Harvard Law School, and if you know a Harvard Law School faculty member and have some working relationship with them, that person's recommendation is very powerful.

On the next tier is an alumnus of the graduate program to which you are applying (not the undergraduate but the graduate program) and also on this tier would be a recommendation from any well-known ("famous") person in the field.

Third in this hierarchy are people with the same credential as you are seeking. For example, if you are applying to law school, then get someone to attest to your ability to get a J.D. from someone who went through the J.D. process rather than a Ph.D. process, and vice versa. A lawyer will have the appropriate perspective – should know what the schools look for in their admitted candidates, as will a Ph.D. in the same field to which you are applying, an M.B.A. holder for business schools, and the like. Your recommendation letter is more likely to touch on the relevant points if it is written by a person who is in the field and understands the qualities the graduate or professional school is seeking.

Q3: When I ask someone to write me a letter, how should I ask? Do I need to provide any information, or should I assume they know what to write?

A3: When you are asking for a letter of recommendation, supply a lot of information in a written form to the letter writer. The writer will utilize that information and say some interesting things about you, above and beyond what they already know about you. They may learn new things about you in the process (your life experience as reflected in your resume, your language abilities or charitable work, etc.) that may impress them and improve what they write about you. You want your letter of recommendation to be very specific, interesting to read and in many ways outstanding. You do not want a bland letter of recommendation saying this person is wonderful and other non-specifics.

Giving your recommender a copy of your resume is the best place to start. And when you give it to them say "here are some examples of things I have done that may assist you in writing a letter of recommendation." You can prioritize what you want them to know.

Normally, in a letter of recommendation, every institution has a different form, but there is a box or option to write something custom-tailored to a specific student, or to use the writer's own letter format. If you are applying to a specialized program, or to a professional graduate school with strengths in a specialized field where your interests lie (e.g., human rights clinic at a law school, non-profit management at an M.B.A. program or Asian studies focus in an international fellowship program, etc.), you should provide a little bit (just a little bit – think brochure, web page print-out, etc.) of information about the particular pro-gram to your recommender. They will then be able to tailor what they say about you to help you convince the admissions staff that you are particularly well-suited to that special program.

Q4: What if I am not sure the person I would like to write my recommendation letters will say positive things about me in the letter?

A4: It is possible that you are not confident about your preferred recommender's ability to recommend you – i.e., you are just not sure if they will say very positive things about you. You can ask them if they are willing to recommend you. They will decline if they cannot say helpful things about you. Usually your worst case scenario is that they cannot say very specific good things, not that they will trash you. Professors and managers usually are honored that you value their opinion and are willing to put your fate in their able hands.

However, if you get the feeling that one person whom you have asked is not terribly enthusiastic, then it might be best to move on and ask someone else who is interested in supporting you. If you are worried that the person you have asked will not focus on the relevant things about you, or cannot write well in the language needed for the letter, then ask politely if you will have an opportunity to see a copy of the letter. You probably cannot request changes, but at least you know what impression you need to compensate for in other parts of your application or interviews.

Q5: Should I ask to see the letter before I send it to the graduate school/employer?

A5: This is a confidentiality issue. Some professors consider letters to be highly confidential and do not want students comparing what they have written in recommendations. Other professors are happy to share a glance at the letter to put the student at ease and may even offer to let you look at the letter without your asking.

Q6: I am a student at an Asian university. I am considering going to graduate school abroad, either in the U.S or U.K. I am worried that my educational background from college would not be as strong as the American and British students who I will be competing with for grades during graduate school. Is this a valid concern?

A6: Unlikely. Take every opportunity to interact with the foreign exchange students and other groups of international people in your community and on your campus so that you will be used to working with people from around the world. This will seem natural after a while, and you will see that your educational background may help you in some ways and may be different or "behind" in others, but probably is not altogether "better" or "worse" overall. Recognize your strengths, try to identify your weaknesses and trust the admissions committees who will accept your application. These committees study the comparative strengths of institutions and are unlikely to make a mistake if they admitted you.

In preparing your application, accentuate the uniqueness of

your background in comparison to other likely applicants. Your foreign cultural and educational background is part of the value you bring to a U.S., U.K. or other overseas campus. You have no rational basis for feeling disadvantaged because you have studied in Asia. The schools here are notorious for working students extremely hard. There is also a good track record showing that Asian students have performed extremely well in many graduate level university programs around the world.

Part IV
Concluding Advice

Chapter 18 Things I Wish I Knew Before My First Job

The advice in the following page is from recent and not-so-recent graduates, reflecting on their experience in their first professional jobs and offering some insights on what they wish they had known before the first day of work. These speeches were given by alumni and professors to current students at Ewha Womans University in Seoul, Korea. They come with sincere wishes to your success and happiness in your early professional sales.

*A. **Advice from an international studies graduate after working for an international non-profit organization for three years**:*

- When you join a company, you have to become a very communicative person. Learn how to e-mail effectively and how to talk over the phone efficiently. If you learn only these two things, you will be more effective and more valuable than you may have expected.
- Be careful about choosing your career field. You can find yourself stuck in the first industry or job field you choose. For example, if you join a marketing company or a marketing team then after several years it can be very hard to move to another field or industry because your skill set is in marketing. So choose an initial job that prepares you for the

field you want. Find a field where you will be happy and successful, given your personal strengths and weaknesses.

- These days, after three or five years, most workers are thinking about moving to other companies. That's very common. Get close to headhunters or other senior consultants or other professionals in other industries or in another field.

B. *Advice from an equity research analyst with a Master's degree in international studies with a concentration in diplomacy and security.*

Background: My education was not an exact match for investment banking, but let me tell you about my background and what I am currently doing. I work in equity research. Very simply, we analyze stocks for investors. I like to think about it as creating investment stories for investors. Our role is to create value opportunities for them when they buy or sell certain stocks. I graduated from my Master's program about a year ago, so I have been working in my role as a research analyst for just about a year. My original plan was to continue studying and get a Ph. D. or go to law school. As a banker (a kind of intermediate strategy for me), I am pleasantly surprised that there is an academic flavor to what we do.

What I wish I had known before I began work:

- Know what kind of technical skill sets you need before you go into the workplace. Something as simple as computer skills will really help you. You have to love Excel (spreadsheets) if you are going to be in finance. I suggest you to start it right now. I have grown to love it, and it is actually quite fun now, after you get some commands down.
- You also have to be very clear in your writing – another technical skill. You don't have to be a perfect writer, but you

have to be a logical writer. I think that's especially important for finance.

- In addition to technical skills, it is important to have a competetive mindset, in whatever field you enter. In investment banking, it is very dangerous to have a casual attitude. There are hundreds of people who want to get a specific position in investment banking. In an investment banking firm, people are very competitive, male and female, even in equity research. More than half of the junior associates are female, and thankfully we all get along. The combination of having a technical skill set and being mentally prepared will really help you in the workplace.
- When you are working at a professional level, time is limited. As a junior, you may have to be in the office before everyone else gets there, and you generally leave after everyone senior leaves. I woke up at 5:30 this morning, took a shower, and got into my car at 6:15. I got to work at about 6:55 to prepare for my 7:30 meeting. This is a very normal day for me. It is not just about seniority, I think, but it is best for your career. As a junior, you get great opportunities to work when you are there for long hours. You learn how to create value for the firm as well as for yourself.
- If you want to have a thriving social life, make lots of friends before you go into investment banking because you are going to lose about half of them once you start working. In terms of significant others, for females, it is very difficult to find the time even for your family. It is probably even more difficult to see your close guy friends. I spend on average maybe 14 to 18 hours in the office. You come into the office on weekends as well. I think for me at this point in time, I am very comfortable with that; in fact, I enjoy it.

C. ***Advice from a year 2000 graduate who has worked as a finance editor, investor relations manager and school administrator*:**

- Workplaces vary from finance to education to international business, but what I want to share is "don't burn your bridges." The international community in Korea, for example, is very small. "Be nice to people on your way up because you will often see them on your way down" – this is true! I ended up working in my first job with some of the friends I had here at school. I have since seen many of my colleagues from my first job at business meetings and various functions in the business community and socially – for example, at professional women's groups. You will see the same people time and time again.
- When you are interviewing, employers do call your references, especially those from people you have worked with. Make sure they have something nice to say about you! I realize that relationships really matter. There was a recent article in the news that said Korean companies value harmony just as much as they value skills. Fortunately or unfortunately, that is the case. People who are very good in dealing with other people often times have advantages in the workplace.
- At the end of the day, it boils down to the value that you add. Although it is important to get along with your colleagues and to make an effort to be a team player, you need to be able to do the work. What I have realized in each of the different positions that I have held over the last seven years is that you really have to work hard. Often, you have to go above and beyond the call of duty. If you look at your job description and you want to fulfill just what is in those lines, you are really short-selling yourself and probably not making

a very good impression on your boss or the organization itself.

- How can you be inspired to rise above the minimum? Take the job and the position that you really care about. Find a mission that you really believe in. I think that is what is going to make you satisfied at the end of the day. And that is I think how you are going to find happiness or success in your job.
- Parents may feel that because they have paid for your education, given you a home and provided all the things you need, they have influence or power over what jobs you choose. Although I think as a good daughter you should of course listen to the counsel of your parents··· I think you also must take a good look at yourself. What type of person are you? What do you like? What makes you happy? What kind of people do you want to be around?
- Take a good look at yourself and do not listen too much or be too pressured by the big names. I don't believe that they are the best fit for all of us. Do not be afraid to take a job with a small non-profit organization that may not pay the big bucks that some of these other companies are paying. Make your choices based on who you want to be. I have seen people take their jobs because of the pressure of their parents wanting them to work for big-name companies. Often, I think they are quite miserable and wish they had chosen otherwise. I feel that life is quite short and you must make choices accordingly.
- I have come to realize that people often quiz you when they first meet you, asking "where did you go to school, where do you work, where do you live" because they are trying to size you up. You should not measure yourself by what other

people think, and certainly not according to what you think other people are measuring. You should measure yourself and others for who they are and what they are contributing to their organizations and to society.

- Ultimately, you have to live according to the choices you make, but you can and should be positive about your choices. In every job that you have there will be times spent doing things like making photocopies or other activities that are not fun. But there is always something that you can learn. Or the people that you work with can sometimes have issues – maybe they are too emotional. But still there is always something that you can learn, and there is always something you can give.
- Sometimes you really do have to make choices to help you balance work and job. They say you can have your cake and eat it, too··· but maybe not all at the same time. Don't be afraid to make the hard choices. Don't always follow the crowd. Ultimately, be true to yourself.

***D. Advice from a manager at an international financial institution who has a Master's degree in international studies*:**

Background: I have four different industries in my career background. First, right after I graduated college, I worked for one of the world's largest electronics firms. Then, I flew all over the world for an international airline for five years. I went to 70 countries and experienced many different places and people from all over the world. Then I decided to go back to school and study more about business with the goal of becoming a banker. Since I had not been in school for years, studying was a new challenge, especially in the beginning. Every other classmate was younger than me. I felt that they were smarter than me and spoke English far better than me. So for me to get used to academics again, I really had to study harder than others. But I just studied a little bit harder than others and my grades improved. I became competitive and it made me feel confident.

After finishing my graduate courses, I worked at a consulting firm specializing in the telecom sector as a research analyst and accounting manager. After a year, I realized my strengths were more in sales and customer relations than the technical aspects of IT/telecoms. I was better at selling the research products to the customers and dealing with company clients, and my sales volume was really good compared to other sales people. So I decided to go into the sales field.

I remembered my earlier interest in investment banking, so I looked for where the investment banking companies were hiring new people. Everybody told me that I am not qualified to be an investment banker and they were mostly right, so I decided to look into commercial banks. Citibank was hiring a sales staff then. The interesting thing for me was that they were hiring sales staff for VIP customers. This work involved acquiring new customers, maintaining them and their assets, and putting together portfolios for their investments. As Citibank was hiring people for that position, I applied for it. Luckily, I was hired on the spot by the interviewer!

Things I wish I'd known:

- Before starting to work in the finance sector, you should know what you really want to do. There are many fields in banking: consumer banking, investment banking, corporate banking, etc. You may really want to do research, which requires you to look at a computer screen a lot, analyzing the numbers, risk factors, corporate management and industries.

If you like to meet people, you can work in sales, where you deal with customers and products available for them like funds, market-linked deposits and other financial products. You can consider if you would like to just do administrative work. If you like MIS (Management Information Systems), and you are good at dealing with numbers, you can work in this area.

- You should know what you really like, what kind of field you want to get into, and what kind of personality and capabilities you have. First, you need to know these things.
- You should make plans, like a candidate running for political office. Write your resume, call the recruiting managers, write impressive letters and use your network. If you know someone who works in the company where you want to work, let yourself and your interest be known to the managers who can hire you.
- Then you should act. If you get a chance to interview, you should really act, like an actor or an actress. You are no longer a recent high school graduate or even a graduate student. You should be really professional, but you should not be too proud of yourself. Confidence and pride are two different things. If you are arrogant, the recruiting manager will not regard you as getting along well with other people or easy to train. However, confidence is a different thing. It is very difficult at first to act confident if you don't feel that way entirely, but you can do it – like an actress at first. Eventually you build enough confidence so that you are not acting anymore. You should learn how to perform so you convey the confident image you want to project.

E. *Advice from a management consultant with an international firm who graduated from university with a degree in international studies last year*:

What I wish I had known before I went to work:

- Before you start working, know what you really want to do. I know it is a difficult question to answer at twenty something, but it is something that you really have to think about. I still don't fully have an answer to that. However, in order to get closer to that answer there was an activity that I joined in college that I will briefly tell you about.
- Even though I am a very quiet person and I am quite shy, some of my friends and I wanted to change some things for the better at our university, so we ended up becoming part of the student council. As student council members, we organized a lot of fun activities. I think through that experience I learned responsibilities that are required in a professional setting. Along with responsibility, I got to learn a lot about communication – how to communicate with groups of students and professors, and how to send a message to a certain group of people.
- Good communication skills will help you and bad communication skills will hurt you. Try to improve your communication skills during college. For example, one of the keys to good communication is realizing what your audience wants to hear from you, and what they expect out of you. How you can find out? You should do a lot of preparation. For instance, before you go to an interview, you can go into the website of the company and read about it.
- This might sound vague and general, but companies spend billions of dollars to develop their values, and then they have

education programs that actually educate employees about the values. You should understand what the company's values are before you go into the interview.

- It's important (in the interview) both to communicate that you're a professional person, and that you are a young professional. In other words, that you are enthusiastic, young, and vibrant; and at the same time, you are someone that can fit into the culture of the company.
- Travel during college. I did. I always felt that I wasn't seeing enough. I always wanted to see the bigger world. My idea was that was if I see more, I can have more options to choose from. Interestingly, the more you see different things, the more you realize what is important to you. I traveled around Europe, the U.S. and Korea, and then, when traveling was not as interesting anymore, I took a semester off during college to go to Africa as a long term volunteer. I think that was one of the turning points in my life, because I came to understand people better while I was there. I realized that wherever you go people are all the same.
- When you interview with someone, you shouldn't be too nervous. My idea of being a good interviewee is being really true to myself. If you are not true to yourself – if you try to convince them you are someone that you are not and you do get into the company, then you will ultimately be very dissatisfied. So I think it is actually better to be true to yourself while you are appearing as a professional person.
- Looking back seven or eight months, I wish I had known more about what I was getting myself into. I did a lot of research before getting the job and thought that I knew what consulting was about. But after I came, I realized there is a lot more responsibility and a lot more stress involved than

my research had revealed. To give you an example, my working hours are usually from about 9 am until 1 or 2 am. That is a typical working day. If there is traffic and I have a client meeting, I may have to get up at 5:30 am. For lunch and dinner, we often order in.

- I was excited about consulting because this is the kind of job where you get to meet a lot of clients and their executives. My expectation level was high. You should have high expectations too, but you have to know that while you work there are disappointments too. Nothing is perfect. That is why it is more important that you actually know what you are getting into. Even if it doesn't link with your final goal, or you are not sure what your final goal is, I think it's meaningful to get work experience as one of the milestones along your path, wherever it leads. Your first job will be OK, even if it is a tough one, if you feel it is part of a track that you are taking to become whatever you want to become.

F. *Advice from a business lawyer after working in law firms for five years*:

- Change may be a constant companion in your professional life. The average number of jobs you may have in your professional career may be more than three. So you have choices to make, and this may be just the beginning of a lifetime of thinking about your career and making changes when the time is right. To be comfortable with change, we are continually career-managing, information-gathering and resisting the temptation to put our heads in the sand.
- You need a first job, not a detailed map of your entire career through retirement. Graduating was the scariest thing I think I confronted. It was terrifying. All my life there had been

school and the opportunity to do more school. I would love to stay in school forever but there is a need and an opportunity to go out into the world and start a professional career. For the first job you only need to have one good thing to do. I think that it's impossible in the early 21st century to look forty years into the future and say I know what I'm going to do, where, and how.

- Take cues from your alumni. At graduation time, I felt that I and many of my classmates had no idea what to do with all our broad-based liberal arts education and legal education. I found that what mattered was that we aimed high and did something interesting for our first jobs. I found that the best resources were people who had been in our positions recently – our alumni group who were out there in the world doing very interesting things.
- Office environments can be a bit of a shock. Some of them are pretty much sensory deprivation chambers – no color, no fresh air. What does it mean to be physically and mentally prepared if you are going to work at an office? Be ready to work on a team. The way to feel comfortable is to get to know the people you work with and become passionate about the work. Most workplaces are not about the physical environment, but the services you provide from that place. The quality and the enjoyment are in the services, in the problem-solving, and in the industry. The office space and desk are not your home, they are just a temporary space for you to use as tools in your mission, whatever that may be.
- Find comic relief at your job. Many first jobs don't involve a leadership position right off the bat. Many first jobs involve document production or research – all good and important things, and jobs that you are well equipped to handle – but

perhaps not so glamorous in the first year.

- You do not have to worry if you are qualified or capable of doing the job. Any job that you are hired to do right out of college or your Master's program is going to be a job you are qualified to do. Once you're hired, just assume you can do this job. So, how do you do this job?
- Get a clear idea of what you are supposed to do narrowly within your job, and also find out how your role fits into the larger mission of your organization.
- Understand and buy into the mission of your organization. This is an important part of happiness for you in that job for however long you are there, whether it's a for-profit company or a charitable or other organization. If you don't believe in the mission, then you should not have joined. The mission of the organization is obviously your first piece of job-search research.

  Some examples: investment banks have a very simple sort of mission: to make money through lending, capital markets services and other banking-related services. For consumer products companies, the mission involves manufacturing and selling certain kinds of products. If you like the products, you are likely to be more naturally enthusiastic about joining the company that produces them. If you think the products are evil, then the company that manufactures and markets them is not the right choice of employer for you. Non-profit organizations mostly have a fairly specific mission like promoting education or providing medical services or other things to underserved markets. Wherever you join up there is a mission. It is important to understand what it is and that you buy into that mission in order to be happy as a part of that mission.

- Join recruiting efforts when you are invited. You will find that you like your employer better when you go out selling its good points to new recruits.
- Make friends at work so you can have people to talk to about the things that are scary or fun or annoying. It is important to be able to let off stress and not take any of it too seriously. In these large organizations, your immediate team and your immediate manager are your world. It is critical to treat those people well and to spend time with those people and learn together.
- Stand up for yourself. You have to be ready to make a case for yourself and your good work. Don't allow your credibility to be undermined. If you have done good work, be confident and take credit where you deserve it.
- Be prepared for what it means to join a large organization with many moving parts and lots of people. In big firms, you are not really the most important thing going on there as a new hire. Your organization is not necessarily designed to support you; you may have to find your own way around it. This is done by talking to people, especially at the social events, so you have a network of contacts around the organization. Find out what the opportunities are within the larger organization you have joined.
- Find a mentor. The most natural person is your immediate supervisor, or a senior person on your immediate team.
- Take heart and realize that ninety percent of success is just showing up. Be at the right place, at the right time. Be prompt and reliable. If you say you will do something at work, they will count on you to make it happen.
- I think that the greatest thing you can do is to get out there and start swimming. You do not need to stay in the

university forever – get out there and grow in the real world. There is no way to bullet-proof yourself, and there is no way to know everything you need to know.

- Live in the moment. You can't start reading now and practicing the specific skills that you are going to need for the first 5 years of a job. Just do a good job at what you are doing right now, and when you get out there you will do a good job for your employer.
- Don't step over an ethical line. Success follows ethical people. It's natural. If you have nothing to hide, you need never feel ashamed. One time could haunt you forever or send you down in flames. If you are true to yourself and you can confidently say, "I gave it my best effort, I did it honestly, I stuck to my principles, and I helped fulfill the mission of the organization that I joined," then you will find your work a rewarding experience.
- Follow your passion.

G. ***Advice from a law professor with a background in investment banking and economics*:**

Background: One of my dreams was to become a lawyer and practice in Asia. Another one of my other dreams was to become an investment banker. First, I was a lawyer for a global investment bank in their Tokyo office. I worked with the best and brightest people, and that was very interesting because they were very sharp, very aggressive people. They were all together at the same place and time to do one thing: make money. Now, that's what I call a very dangerous combination, in a good sense.

Even though I am a licensed lawyer in the United States, I wanted to be on the business side. In other words, to create value for the firm – make money as part of the trading desk (where they really bring in the money for the bank). Banks need profits to survive, and it's made in the front office by the traders: bond traders, structured products traders, and foreign exchange traders. After working for several years in Tokyo as a lawyer, I was recruited to work on the business side in Hong Kong. After some time in Hong Kong, I finally joined this institution here in Seoul. It's quite a trip, in terms of starting off in Tokyo, going to Hong Kong, and ending up here in Korea. I did all of this without any personal connections, so if I can do it, then I think all of you guys can do it too. I had to figure out how to leverage what I learned in the classroom to get a job, make some money to buy things that I wanted, and do the things that I wanted to do.

Reflections on Google: Recently, I came upon with some facts related to Google. Google is a premier web search engine. It is quickly replacing a lot of things that people used to do in terms of finding information. Previously, it took days to find out a fact; nowadays, in just a few seconds, you can come up with the information about anything, anywhere, at any place and time. It is very powerful. Guess what are the top three global searches on Google? Why don't you say what the first one is? I will give you a hint: starts with S, it has three letters, one word: sex. That is not the topic of today's conversation. The second most frequently searched word in the world according to Google is also a three letter word. It starts with "g." It is also the name of a Korean pop band. God. And number three, the third most searched word for Google is a four letter word, starts with "J." Jobs. So you have people looking for jobs, god, maybe praying to god for a job, maybe praying to god for something else, but anyway these are the three top searches.

Jobs are not only on your minds, but on other people's minds.

That is both good and bad news. It is good news that you are thinking about them, but it is bad news that a lot of people in the rest of the world are also thinking about them too. They are the people you have to compete with, head to head. It is as hard to get into some employers as it is to get into a top university.

So, strategically speaking, the question is, how do you make it happen? I will give you my top five recommendations or insights in reverse order, in terms of what I wish I had known before I started my career.

- Number Five: Appearances matter. In the idealistic classroom, if you get the material, get the right score on the test and say the right things, it doesn't really matter what you look like. You can be an individual. At work, you represent your company. You may be the individual put on the front line, meeting clients, working with other people in the firm to create client relationships, and dealing with people from outside the company.
    - In that new role, appearances matter – form matters – just as much as, maybe more than, substance. So, how do you make that happen? How do you make sure you create a positive appearance? Dress sharp, think sharp, and talk sharp. When you talk sharp, I mean, speak concisely, exactly. Choose exactly the right words; think before you speak. Make every word count. Dressing sharply, well, just be professional and dress conservatively, not over the top.
    - What is over the top? I interviewed lots of people and dealt with lots of resumes in Tokyo and in Hong Kong. For the resume, we try to figure out who is qualified, and who we want to spend five minutes chatting with in an interview. Once we bring the candidate into the boardroom or conference room for an interview, some things signal what

kind of person they might be or, what kind of character they may have. Some signals scream "don't hire me": a flashy, expensive watch, like a Rolex.

- o Why? It signals to me and to others that this candidate may not want to work, that she has led a privileged life. A watch that costs a huge percentage of the first year's salary signals the person is used to getting things handed to them. You want to be seen as hungry, willing to work and fight for the company. Companies and managers look for attitude. Similar comment on cufflinks for men and handbags for women: Gucci, Channel, etc. signal the same thing. Top firms want people who are smart, aggressive and nice to work with; not spoiled, not people who think they are owed something. That's why appearances matter.
- o Also, be nice to everyone. Whether you like them or not, whether you disagree with them or not, whether you don't like the way they talk, they look, their skin color – be nice. There's an expression, "be nice to everyone on your way to the top, because you'll see them on your way down."

- Number Four: You must fight for your rights. You will have to fight for your rights many times. This may not be on your radar screen yet, but it needs to be once you start working. About your bonus, for example: when you work in investment banking, they may pay you fifty or a hundred thousand dollars a year, but it is a true free market capitalist system based on greed and you may need to fight for a bonus that can be two or three times your annual salary. I used to think before I started working, "Hey, if I'm a nice guy, if I just do my job, and I keep quiet, then I'll get the bonus that I deserve." Reality is different. You really have to fight for your bonus. Promotions are the same thing.

o I also thought that if I do a good job and come in at certain hours and just do what I am told then I will get promoted after a certain amount of time. Well, unless you work for the government that is probably not going to happen. You get promoted based on your ability, your "value added" to a firm. Don't keep the status quo. To be too "stable" is actually to lose ground in terms of professional advancement. As time goes on, you broaden your experience and your skill sets. If you don't, that may signal to you that you may not be at the right firm, right time, doing the right thing.

o Everyone, I firmly believe, is intelligent. If you are not succeeding in your particular institution, that does not mean you are dumb, stupid, or unqualified. It probably means that it is just not a good fit for you. Once you find the right fit, then you will create a lot of value, do a lot of great things, be happy, make your boss happy, and then everyone will be happy.

o How to make this happen? How do you fight for your bonus? How do you fight for your position? How do you fight to get added coverage? Make your thoughts known. Don't be quiet. Express what is on your mind. How you express it is just important. When you express what you say, think about it clearly. Most people don't remember long sentences or long speeches about what you should do or what you deserve. Keep it short.

o In marketing and PR, most slogans are three or four words maximum. Campaigns, political campaigns are three or four words maximum. Why? Because that's all people remember at the end of the day. So, when you make your case, put three or four things to your boss. Say "listen, these are the three or four things that I worked on, that I was responsible for, that I fought for to make you look good, and that's why I deserve this bonus and this promotion. That is why I deserve it." This is very important. Don't be overly aggressive, just be confident, be professional, be clear.

- Number Three: I call it "practice the Eliot Spitzer rule." Eliot Spitzer is a lawyer. He also happens to be the attorney general for the state of New York. And in my view he is probably one of the most brilliant people in the world. He is also very powerful. So what is this Eliot Spitzer rule? It applies once you start working. When you are a student, you love to write text messages, don't you? You love to chat, you like to send e-mails. But once you start working that is risky. Putting stuff down on paper and in writing is very risky because it creates evidence.
  - o Reflecting that, Eliot Spitzer says, "Never write, when you can speak." Once you put something down on paper, it is memorialized forever and can be used for litigation, against you or your firm. Next, "Never speak, when you cannot." Right? When you speak and you say something, you're taking a position. That means fifty percent of the people may disagree with you and your position. So instead of speaking, just nod. Oh, that person nodded. This way or that way? I just nodded, may be I had an itch, or just stretching – they can't blame me for that! So, never write when you can speak, and never speak when you cannot. Finally, "Never ever, put anything in an e-mail." Why? E-mails go back and forth, between co-workers, and clients, and can be stored forever and retrieved even if you deleted them.

- o Speaking of e-mails, I think that one communication problem for many junior workers is e-mail overuse. Sometimes e-mail traffic is longer than the traffic in Gangnam (Seoul) and Los Angeles put together – it goes on for pages and pages, and it goes nowhere. E-mail can be a problem if it creates more issues than it solves. There is something called a telephone. You may have forgotten about it – it was invented a hundred years ago. You pick it up, you talk to a person, and you can hear their voice and exchange thoughts. There is an expression: a picture is worth a thousand words. I think one phone call is worth a hundred e-mails. Pick up the phone, talk to someone, and it will save you a lot of time while it creates a better relationship with the other person.

- Number Two: Don't forget the big picture. One of the false steps that many junior workers make is thinking inside their own personal box: "I cover this client, I cover this type of trade, this is what I do, and if I do it very well, I'll get promoted and be recognized." But that is not always the case. Most of the time if you do your job, and cover your area well you can be proud of it. Do it with passion, because people will notice that passion. But, from time to time, separate yourself from the pack and make yourself unique (but not strange). Stand out as exceptional but don't stick out as abnormal.
  - o Think of your coverage area as the tree. If you focus only on one tree (leaves, branch, bark), you may forget that any your tree is surrounded by thousands of trees (the forest). If you do not grasp the big picture, you are likely to be in that same box for your entire career with that firm. But managers are looking for people who (i) do their job very

well, and on top of that, (ii) see the big picture. That is people who see how what they are doing relates to what the firm and the department are trying to do now and in the future. In that way, private sector companies are not like government departments.

- Companies are offensive machines. They must compete in markets and are looking for their competitive advantage, for new products and new clients. They won't succeed if their employees are just sitting in a box, doing the same job today as they did five years ago. So, get out there at lunch time and after work to have drinks and lunch with people who you don't know that well. Yes, you will continue to have your inner circle of friends with whom you are comfortable. But also move around, meet some new people, and get some new perspectives.
- When you are at lunch and talking with these people, engage them and learn what you can. The smartest people in the world don't spend their time lecturing other people. Actually, when they speak, they gain information as much or more than they give. Try to get a net inflow of information. When you speak with other people, for example, ask them questions: What is your job? What are your opinions on this? How do you see your firm growing in the future, your division? What do you think of my role, my division? How can I create better value? When you get their opinion, of course you don't have to accept it. But at least you're engaging them, so you get information. They will be more cooperative with you in the future because they know you – you are creating allies. So, engage everyone, ask their opinions.
- Another person I admire very much, Robert Rubin, is also

a lawyer and an investment banker. In the 1960s, after practicing law for just a short time, he joined a small investment bank that was relatively unknown. He went into risk arbitrage, which means that he would look at the global markets and find an opportunity (some lasting for just a few minutes) where you can buy in one market and sell the same thing in another market for a higher price. It is a complex and stressful job, but he did it well. He moved up the ranks in that firm (Goldman Sachs), eventually becoming co-president. Then he was asked by President Clinton in the 1990s to become the U.S. Treasury Secretary.

o If you recall your economic history, the 1990s was a critical time with a series of financial crises – the Mexican peso, the Russian ruble and the Asian financial crisis. He managed all that, helping to minimize the damage. After serving as Treasury Secretary, Rubin later joined Citigroup in New York. The first thing he did at Citigroup was go around meeting all the people he would work with (higher, same level, and lower); he took a yellow pen and pad, and he just asked questions, such as, "What is your expectation of my job?," "What would you like me to do?," "How about your job? What do you do?," and "How can we do it better?" Immediately, he had no enemies. He got a bunch of people to see him as a colleague, not as a political foe. And he learned a lot about the firm, just by talking to a few people. He probably had a good time talking to people, very smart and intelligent people. Never forget the big picture.

- Number One: Sun Tzu was a great Chinese war strategist. Over a thousand years ago, he wrote "The Art of War." In the Art of War, he had lots of good advice on how to win and when to engage your enemies. One of the many quotable things he said is "Keep your friends close, but keep your enemies closer." You can trust your friends – you don't have to watch them all the time; but your enemies – you have to be very careful to know what they are plotting. That's why Kissinger and Nixon, in the 1970s, engaged Russia and China. Because those nations were perceived as enemies, the Americans engaged those countries to figure out what they were up to, determine what they were thinking, and learn their strategy and motivations.

- o A related point for job-seekers is: "Keep your friends close, but keep your headhunters closer." Headhunters create efficient labor markets. They match up supply and demand. You have the demand, and hiring companies have the supply. It's fairly difficult for you to find each other, so headhunters help by matching you up. You can get to know the headhunters in your field, and it will definitely help you, as it helped me and many other people I know in the fields of banking, consulting, law and other professions.

- Don't be afraid. You may think that your future is uncertain, and it may be. But once in a while you have to shoot for the stars. Shoot for your dreams and follow your passion. You may miss 99 out of 100. But guess what? Maybe one time, you will hit one of the stars. And that is all it takes to launch your global career and become a "master of the universe."

Chapter 19 Additional Resources

Many good resources are available online. The best source of information is the company's or school's own website. As a second source, look for the rankings and industry reviews of the institutions you are considering. When you become focused on particular companies or schools, talk to people who have graduated from, currently attend or currently work there to get current, first-hand information.

Worthwhile resources have been listed at the end of the each section of this volume for guidance in relating to the first professional job and graduate schools. Additionally, the following materials are available from a good on-campus career resource library or major English-language bookseller:

***Job Hunting, Resume and Interviews*:**

10 Things Employers Want You to Learn in College by Bill Coplin (Ten Speed Press 2003).

Get the Interview Every Time – Fortune 500 Hiring Professionals' Tips for Writing Winning Resumes and Cover Letters by Brenda Greene

International Job Finder: Where the Jobs are Worldwide by Daniel Lauber (Planning/Communications, 2003)

International Jobs Directory by Ron and Caryl Krannich (Impact Publications, 1999).

International Jobs: Where They Are, How to Get Them by Nina Segal & Eric Kocher (Basic Books 2003).

Job Interviews for Dummies by Joyce Lain Kennedy (Hungry Minds, 2000)

Kick Off Your Career – Write a Winning Resume, Ace Your Interview, Negotiate a Great Salary by Kate Wendleton (Career Press, 2002).

Monster Careers – How to Land the Job of Your Life by Jeff Taylor (Penguin Books 2004).

What color is your parachute? – A practical manual for job-hunters and career-changers by Richard N. Bolles (Ten Speed Press 2005).

Career Planning

The Global Citizen by Elizabeth Kruempelmann (Ten Speed Press 2002).

How to Live Your Dream of Volunteering Overseas by Joseph Collins (Penguin Books, 2002).

Life Strategies – Doing What Works, Doing What Matters by Phillip C. McGraw (Hyperion 1999).

Life's Greatest Lessons – 20 Things that Matter by Hal Urban (Fire Side 2003).

Now, Discover Your Strengths by Marcus Buckingham/Donald O. Clifton (Free Press 2001).

The Success Principles – How to Get from Where You are to Where you Want to Be by Jack Canfield (Harper Collins 2005).

What should I do with my life? The True Story of People Who Answered the Ultimate Question by Po Bronson (Random House 2003).

Vault Career Guide to International Careers by Sally Christie and the staff of Vault (Vault Inc. 2004)

Business

Harvard Business Review on Women in Business (Harvard Business School Press 2005).

What can you do with a major in Business? Real People, Real Jobs, Real Rewards by Kate Shoup Welsh (Wiley 2005).

International Affairs

Careers in International Affairs, Seventh Edition School of Foreign Service, Georgetown University, 2003.

Guide to Careers in World Affairs by Foreign Policy Association, 1993.

Law

Careers in International Law, American Bar Association by Mark W. Janis, 1993.

Directory of Opportunities in International Law by John Bassett Moore Society of International *Law* (Charlottesville, Virginia, 1992).